Anna MAN

INTERNET JUSTICE

Philosophy of Law

for the Virtual World

BUENOS BOOKS AMERICA

ISBN: 1-932848-08-8 (PAPERBACK)
ISBN: 1-932848-09-6 (E-BOOK)

English and Spanish versions published by:

BUENOS BOOKS AMERICA
BuenosBooksAmerica@BuenosBooksAmerica.com
http://www.buenosbooksamerica.com

French version published by:
Buenos Books International (Paris)
www.BuenosBooks.com
BuenosBooks@BuenosBooks.com

FRENCH PAPERBACK: ISBN 2915495106
FRENCH E-BOOK: ISBN 2915495092
SPANISH PAPERBACK: 1-932848-00-2
SPANISH E-BOOKS: 1-932848-01-0
English version previously published by the University
Press of America (ISBN: 0-7618-2378-6) under the title:
Ancient Egyptian Wisdom for the Internet.

CAUTION: Please do not photocopy this book. Buy
the electronic version instead: cheap, convenient and meets
the author's rights.

E-books available on our Websites:

WWW.BUENOSBOOKSAMERICA.COM
WWW.BUENOSBOOKS.COM

ii

CONTENTS

iii

iv

PREFACE

The world of ideas, so cherished by Plato, is made available to the human mind as much by the Internet as by pictorial design or the written word. The novelty introduced by the Internet is not virtuality in itself, but only the extended power to free ideas from the physical constraints of space, time and the material world in general, as well as from censorship.[1] Thus, the entire mental world of modern man can display itself on the Internet, and all kinds of ideas, information and pictures can be emitted. Therefore, it can come as no surprise to find the dark side of the human psyche as well as the expression, sometimes crude and perverted, of its universal attraction to sexuality, disseminated throughout this new form of virtuality. The expression of sexual perversion and the development of electronic commerce are the two main excuses invoked by states for their legal intervention. Unfortunately, bound as it is by geographical limits, governmental regulation is ill-adapted to the worldwide dimension of the Internet: globalization increasingly impedes the efficiency of national laws. Moreover, a wide majority of Internet users rejects any legal intrusion into this space, conceived essentially as a realm of thought and fantasy, free from constraint. They argue that the Internet has developed and expanded without the help of legal authorities. Why should governments disturb a world that has no use for them, and which has profited so much from its freedom? Some people answer that laws have become necessary due to the many abuses now existing in cyberspace. They believe states should intervene to protect, say, privacy or the rights of authors, both of which seem to be seriously threatened by the Internet. With greater originality, one author[2] states that, as the Internet is becoming a space where the technological "code" (software) designed by industrial "authorities", is effectively substituting itself for law, citizens should possess control over this new kind of hidden legal power. He believes that citizens should be made aware of this evolution of the Net and should be able to choose, as they do in the "real" world, the values they want to promote. Which values should we choose? American constitutional values?[3] Chinese values? Indian or French values? If we put the question this way, we inevitably fall back on the positive law of a given state. But any such choice is once again confronted by the extra-national dimension of the Internet. An adaptation of old national laws to new circumstances no longer serves any purpose: we must be more creative, as Lawrence LESSIG observed.[4] As cyberspace and real space function differently, they cannot implicate the same legal values. The most elementary wisdom invites us to forget our legal past, so obviously ill-adapted to the Internet, so as to gain a better insight into the functioning of virtual space. Attempts to regulate the Internet in the same way as the real world have inevitably failed and will continue to fail. The only solution that can foster the expansion of the net and justify state intervention will come from a philosophy of law suited to virtuality. Our philosophical legal traditions stemmed from agricultural and industrial roots and are therefore widely useless within the virtual context. They cannot help us - but the philosophy of ancient civilizations can. At first sight, it may seem paradoxical to look to ancient civilizations for counsel on legal regulation of the Internet. But the virtual world is not a modern invention. It has existed for ever; although we previously tended to ignore it because it did not seem to be of great economic value. The development of electronic commerce is now opening our eyes to the economic power of the intangible world. Ancient Egypt and Rome did not have the Internet, but they were aware of the importance of an intangible world. They accurately observed the functioning of that world and used their knowledge of it in the legal field. The Ancient Egyptians invented an original and useful concept of "virtual justice" whose aim was to create prosperity. The very practical ancient Romans noticed an overlap between virtuality and matter, and they used this overlap in the foundation of their legal system.[5] *Internet Justice* demonstrates that the legal philosophy and knowledge of these two ancient civilizations are of great value in helping us deal with the Internet.

INTRODUCTION

Recent attempts from many governments proved the inefficiency of the traditional legal ruling in the context of the Internet. Even slightly modified the existing laws are unsuitable. Why? In order to find an answer to this question we must closely observe the modern positive legal systems. This way, we will be able to perceive the main features of these systems more clearly in order to confront them with the Internet's virtual world. The essential features of the modern positive legal systems turn mainly:

- on one side, around the concept of territory, without which positive laws cannot work, while this concept is on the contrary totally out of purpose in the virtual world;
- on the other side, around the essential distinction between things and persons. Positive laws are mainly focused on sharing material things and on dealing with the right of property. The Internet is focused on the personal side of life, and on the creativity and prosperity coming from persons and not from things. The legal distinction between things and persons was already used by the ancient Roman Lawyers when they invented the distinction between the

action in rem and the *actio in personam*. During the sixteenth century, with the emergence of the concept of subjective rights, this distinction was mistranslated in continental legal systems. It was rendered by the unclear legal distinction between real (material) subjective right (droit réel subjectif) and personal subjective right (droit personnel subjectif) which is still effective. The first part of the work seeks to clarify the fundamental differences between cyberspace and "real" space. We shall examine in chapter 1 the ensuing consequences of the concept of territory. In the second chapter we shall examine the differences between cyberspace and real space emerging from their respective focus on matter and on persons. The second part of the book describes the pragmatic approach taken by the ancient Roman lawyers to the virtual world, an approach that sheds light on some several important Internet-related issues. The third part explores the ancient Egyptian concept of justice. Finally the work applies that concept to the Internet

PART 1

FUNDAMENTAL DIFFERENCES

BETWEEN

CYBERSPACE AND REAL SPACE

Anna Mancini

CHAPTER 1

EARTHLY LIFE AND VIRTUAL WORLD

In this chapter we shall see how the Earth and the concept of territory play a fundamental role in the traditional legal world,[6] while they do not matter within the Internet. Due to this lack of territory-based architecture, the whole traditional legal process becomes inefficient in cyberspace. A traditional legal world so deeply linked to the Earth since its origins can only lose its bearings and feel confused when confronted with a virtual world deprived of territories and borders.

1. Basic instinct and legal territoriality

The philosopher Jean-Jacques ROUSSEAU, in his book entitled: *Discourse On The Origin Of Inequality*[7] stressed the link between political organization and the ownership of land,[8] as follows:

The true founder of civil society was the first man who, having enclosed a piece of land, thought of saying, 'This is mine', and came across people simple enough

3

to believe him. How many crimes, wars, murders and how much misery and horror, the human race might have been spared if someone had pulled up the stakes or filled in the ditch, and cried out to his fellows: 'Beware of listening to this charlatan. You are lost if you forget that the fruits of the earth belong to all and that the earth itself belongs to no one!'

If it is obvious that the need for land appropriation is one of the most striking features of the human being, this is not only a human instinct. This need is also shared by other realms of life. Any kind of life on the Earth is so dependent on the Earth, often called "mother-Earth", that fights for land appropriation do not only concern human beings. Plants, for example, fight in varied ways for a territory. This fact was finely described by the botanist Jean-Marie PELT.[9] The same occurs too in the animal realm.[10] Primarily, Earth appeared to ancient civilizations to be a living being.[11] Being a living entity Earth was venerated, respected and the object of varied cults. Some people still consider it to be sacred and out of the sphere of commercial transactions. In the Canadian Aboriginal peoples' Charter of the Earth, we can read the following sentences, very illustrative of the link these populations have with the Earth:[12]

The native peoples have been placed upon our mother Earth, by the Creator. We belong to the Earth. We

4

cannot be severed from our lands and territories. Our territories are living entities forming part of the permanent vital link between the human beings and nature.

The Lakota Indian Noble Red Man speaks as follows in a very evocative manner:[13]

Only god is our father, and the Earth is our mother. Being of the same color as our Mother-Earth, our skin proves it.

This same kind of respect for the land and also for the spirits deemed to possess it can be found in the minds of other peoples like the Sara of the South of Chad, studied by Jean-Pierre MAGNANT.[14] The author wrote an interesting thesis in which he studied the legal and political organization of this people. He explains how different from the French colonizers was the native people's approach to the Earth.[15] This people believes that the lands belong to spirits. As a result, if a human group wants to live on a piece of land, this can only be done after having passed an agreement with the spirits of the place. It is the priest of the Earth who passes the agreement, he who knows the appropriate rituals[16] and owns the magical objects.[17] The village will then settle on the lands ritually given by gods. In exchange for this gift, the people will follow the rules flowing from the initial agreement, i.e.: compliance with the

5

custom and accomplishment of the appropriate rituals.[18] It is therefore easy to understand that as lands are the property of gods, nobody can totally possess them except gods, hence nobody can sell them. The people of a village only have the right to use the lands of their settlement. In such a cultural context, it is logical that lands cannot be sold and bought, as nobody owns them, except gods. The power of man on lands is a very limited one, strictly dependent on the full power of the spirits of the place.[19] As gifts to human beings from gods, the lands are sacred and nobody actually owns them.[20]

Lands are in fact collectively possessed through the gods.[21] This people treats the lands with respect and preserves them for new generations. A piece of land cannot be the property of a specific man, land is not a common object that can be possessed. Gods never give the land to one man only, but to the whole village, which is made of living beings as well as ancestors and future generations.[22] In these societies, as in the western modern world, the way we deal with the land shapes the political structure of society. A society where the Earth is sacred cannot by definition be organized the same way as a society where lands are not sacred and can therefore be sold and bought, and be natural objects of business. Nevertheless, the Earth in both societies plays the major role in the social organization because land is one of the fundamental needs of living beings (human, plant or animal). The instinct that links us to our nourishing Earth is so strong, so primordial, that it is not surprising to notice that all the existing legal positive systems are structured "around the Earth". Today land still plays a major role in all the branches of law and especially in International Law. Civil law, criminal law, business law, as well as copyright law, are all structured around the earthly concepts of land, space, place, territory, boundaries etc... Even KELSEN's *Pure Theory of Law* does not escape this strong link with the Earth. It is in fact totally constructed with the key-concepts of place, space, link between time and space, and also around the concept of territory which is totally irrelevant within the Internet. After a personal presentation of Hans KELSEN's theory, we shall see how in the Internet the default of this element -so dear to the human psyche and so deeply rooted in the collective unconscious- makes lawyers feel lost. For the first time in history, the most ancient and fundamental legal bearings have become useless. Hence, how can lawyers justify the application within the Internet of laws and of a legal philosophy built and focused on the territory criterion when this criterion is irrelevant in cyberspace?

2. Territory as the masterpiece of legal positivism

Present day legal systems -whether they belong to the continental system, to common law or whether they are comprehended in religious systems- were all originally and gradually built upon the longing for justice. It is such a need that gave the impulse to create as just a society as possible. Despite this basic longing for justice, a legal philosophy ignoring this need has emerged in the western world and has culminated in Hans KELSEN's *Pure Theory of Law*.[23] This author considers himself to be the heir of the nineteenth century legal positivism the aim of which he simply continued through purifying the law of all its ideological features.[24] However Hans KELSEN's heritage appears to be far more ancient and can be traced back to the invention of writing. In fact, if lawyers can today consider the law to be a science of the normative architecture, they can do it only because we live in a civilization of written word. Through successive legal strata, writing allowed the building of legal systems focused on texts and not on justice. Of course, such a kind of legal system could not exist in so called primitive verbal civilizations. Within them, legal innovation was made compulsory, as lawyers or priests acting as lawyers could not refer to a written memory containing the "ready to use" solutions. The search for a fair solution was in this context the only means to balance social life. In the actual continental legal systems, lawyers can refer to a set of written solutions embodied in texts like: Declarations of Human Rights, the written constitutions, and the codifications -since 1804 for France and later on for other countries-. All these written sources formed the basic ground without which Hans KELSEN's *Pure Theory of Law* would never have existed. In order to understand the *Pure Theory of Law* better it is useful to set it back in its historical context. The first German publication of the *Pure Theory of Law* occurred in 1934 after the first world war. The French translation was published at the end of the second world war.[25] In this context, we can understand the will of Hans KELSEN to purify law from ideology as ideology seems to lead to war. But Hans KELSEN goes much further: he purifies its legal system of general ideology,[26] political ideology,[27] morality[28] and of the ideal of justice.[29] He turned the study of legal systems into a neutral science,[30] a tool, a technique. But if we follow the author's rationale, law can be used the way desired by any kind of power serving any kind of ideology.[31] Isn't it paradoxical to purify the law of ideologies and in so doing to turn it in a blind tool which can serve the ends of any kind of ideology? Hence, what we can deduce is that the two world wars strongly led Hans KELSEN to mistrust the human feelings which are to him the cause of ideology and therefore of war. In consequence, in order to prevent such bad effects of human emotions he built a legal science purified of any kind of (dangerous) sentimentality. He turned legal science in a neutral, abstract objective and logical science. Hans KELSEN said that the *Pure Theory of Law* was seeking the truth and was against (false) ideology.[32] Due mainly to the fact that the *Pure Theory of Law* shows legal science under a serious logical mask, Hans KELSEN's theory has been considerably successful. Both the *Pure Theory of Law* and natural sciences are purified of ideologies. One knows that such a purification

9

allowed natural sciences to achieve significant progress. Moreover, another advantage is that the Law being a science, the lawyers, like the scientists, will not be held responsible for the misuse of legal tools. Their sole aim is progress, ideologies are out of their purpose. As the ideology of justice stems from human sentimentality, justice cannot be one of the purposes of legal science. Hans KELSEN criticizes the lawyers ignoring the actual purpose of legal science.[33] According to the author the sole role of jurists is to know the law and to describe it through legal norms.[34] The author considers that the jurists must only deal with legal norms. Justice, morals or politics are not part of their purpose. The same is also valid for the judge who must not question the fairness of a legal norm.[35] In conclusion there is obviously no space in legal science for the concept of justice. This is also true for the current legal positivism. As the idea of justice stems from a subjective human feeling, Hans KELSEN believes it must be excluded from the sphere of legal science. Being scientific, legal science must possess the essential characteristic of natural sciences. It must therefore be objective, logical and obedient to scientific laws, taking in Hans KELSEN's theory the name of "legal rules" (règles juridiques).[36] While imitating natural sciences, Hans KELSEN gives to legal science the appearance of objectivity and rationality that made the success of natural sciences. In doing so he replaces the (objective) principle of causality of the natural science with an (objective) legal principle of imputation.[37] Moreover, according to the author, the legal science as well as natural sciences is objective because it applies to external objects which can be rationally described and studied. Legal norms are the external objects on which legal science can be efficiently built, while the concept of justice and its opposite cannot be objective and hence cannot be taken as external objects studied by legal science.[38]

Purified in such a way of morals, politics, justice and any kind of ideology, legal science deals solely with norms and national or international pyramidal hierarchies of norms. Legal norms or legal rules are all without exception linked to the existence of the territoriality criterion, which they cannot escape. This is the reason why the concept of territoriality is the masterpiece of the *Pure Theory of Law*. Contrary to what occurs in legal systems focused on the search for fair solutions, the concepts of space, location or territory play a major role in KELSEN's theory. Hans KELSEN often use the formula "in space and in time"[39] or "in a specific place". He writes for example: "The connection of the norm to space and time is its spatial and temporal sphere of validity."[40] According to Hans KELSEN, without an earthly link no effective legal norm can exist insofar as:

The norm must, then, also determine in its content both where and when the behavior takes place -or, in terms of the norm, 'ought to take place'. The validity of norms governing human behavior generally (an so, the validity of legal norms in particular) is spatial and temporal validity because these norms have as their content spatial and temporal events. That a norm is valid will always mean that it is valid in some space or another and for some time or another -in other words, that it refers to events that can only take place somewhere and at some time.[41]

The last chapter of the *Pure Theory of Law* shows how essential the criterion of territoriality (or of space) is to legal positivism and to International Law. There, Hans KELSEN explains that a State is not a "legal person" but only a set of laws,[42] the validity of which for a given territory provides the condition of its existence. Therefore, without a territory,[43] a State (considered as a legal system) cannot exist and cannot be internationally recognized. According to the author a State is a legal order[44] applying to a given territory. In International Law a State will be considered as a valid State only if the legal set of laws it personifies is effective on a given territory.[45] What is essential is not the way a State was formed but the efficacy of its legal system through the efficacy of legal coercion on a given territory. Through a so-called scientific demonstration KELSEN denies any kind of sovereignty to states.[46] He believes the concept of sovereignty to be only the result of ideologies and especially of a primitive ideology which has nothing to do within a pure legal science.[47] KELSEN esteems that

International Law will move toward more centralization,[48] which will make it less primitive. Anyway, despite the traditional approach to International Law, the author claims that the concept of the sovereignty of states must be overcome.[49] The sole valid criterion will be the criterion of the efficacy of the State viewed as a pyramidally constructed legal set. KELSEN demonstrates that whichever starting point we take (State or International Law) no State sovereignty can exist.[50] Indeed KELSEN's logic is very simple, if one understands that a State is not a legal person but only a set of laws effective on a given territory, how can such a set of laws have any kind of sovereignty normally dedicated to persons? The main characteristic of a state (or of a set of norms which is identical) is its spatial and temporal effectiveness. KELSEN writes:

> The territory of the individual State, which is the spatial sphere of validity of the State legal system, extends - because of international law- as far as the legal system is effective. And international law guarantees this territorial sphere of validity by attaching its specific consequences (reprisal or war) to the unlawful act of an intrusion into the area under its protection.[51]

Through the many examples given, it is clear that a positivistic approach to law cannot under any circumstances escape the territory criterion. The reason why we presented Hans KELSEN's positivistic legal theory (which has been criticized by scholars who opened new horizons to law)[52] is because it is an excellent and almost caricatured illustration of the necessary link between all the current modern legal systems and the territory criterion. Just remove the concept of territory and the positivistic *Pure Theory of Law* can no longer exist. The erosion of the role played by the territory criterion is today the reason for the "crisis of territoriality" faced by the International Law and that we are now going to explain.

3. Territoriality crisis in the contemporary International Law

Contrary to Hans KELSEN, the majority of writers in the field of International Law recognizes the sovereignty of states.[53] Nevertheless the idea of the necessary link between the concept of State and that of territory is shared not only by Hans KELSEN, but also by the majority of scholars specializing in International Law. They all believe that states cannot exist without a territory.[54] For example, Maurice FLORY, when speaking about the couple State-territory[55] underlines the inevitable intermingling between the concepts of State and territory.[56] Faced with the idea of the "international without territory", some simply deny the crisis in the International Law in regard to the concept of territory.[57] Marcel MERLE, for example, cannot resign himself to the disappearance of this fundamental legal

1 4

criterion.[58] Taking the often mentioned example of the multinational companies some authors argue that far from having become useless, the concept of territory is very useful in this context. These companies take advantage of the existence of territories and of the diversity of laws they involve. Hence, the existence of distinct territories forms a major part of their strategic thinking.[59] According to some international lawyers, there is not a real crisis of territoriality, but only a change in perspective due to the significant increase in international exchanges. Such a change makes the control operated by the states more difficult, but does not constitute an attempt on their sovereignty within their territories. But these writers generally notice that states have now to increase their international cooperation for a more effective management of their own territories. According to a great number of scholars there is no crisis of territoriality in the International Law and hence states and their laws are not in crisis. This opinion is not shared by some other scholars who assert that the International Law based upon territorial divisions is in crisis.[60] In effect, it is easy to notice the two following points:

1°) Insofar as operations on material goods can be located in time and space, no crisis of territoriality can actually be noticed as long as we deal with material goods.

2°) On the contrary, as soon as human activities become both immaterial and worldwide, it is no longer possible to speak of a crisis of territoriality. Territory in such a context simply does not matter. An excellent example is the international financial market studied by Wladimir ANDREFF.[61] He demonstrates the extent to which states have nowadays lost their sovereignty over their own territory regarding the monetary circulation. According to the author, in the field of international finance there are no longer territories. He cannot now imagine how it can be possible to regulate this field of human activities otherwise.[62] If it is true that in the field of finance the efficiency of the territorial criterion has gradually decreased, in the Internet this criterion has never existed. Despite the lack of such a territorial criterion within the Internet, lawyers and governments continue attempting to apply to the Internet rules and attitudes fitted to a world divided into territories.

4. The crash of the territoriality criterion in cyberspace

4. 1: Internet-related freedom

By the end of the nineties, the economists were already speaking of cyber-economy. They referred in more general terms to the economy of information.[63] Such a cyber-economy included financial transactions (which became global and immaterial) as well as television, radio, or telephony.[64] It was already true that media like satellite television made the principle of territoriality[65] ineffective. Indeed, how can a State manage to impose any kind of rule upon a television channel established in a foreign territory but emitting its programs through satellite on its own territory? Within the Internet, the inefficiency of the traditional protections offered by boundaries is increased. One of the reasons for this is that the Internet multiplies the number of actors who can take advantage of the ineffectiveness of boundaries. These actors are no longer only the multinational companies (media, or finance necessarily working at an international level due to the globalization of economy[66]) but also small businesses as well as individuals. Within the Internet individuals now have the opportunity to be more than passive receivers of information. They can also create information and emit it worldwide. They do not need to be as big as the traditional characters (states, Non Governmental Organizations, multinational companies and banks, etc...) of the international world in order to exist in this dimension. As it cuts down the costs of international communication and considerably decreases the time necessary to reach a great number of people spread throughout the world, the Internet allows anyone to diffuse information worldwide and also to escape to a certain extent the traditional constraints of the home territory. The Internet now prevents states from completely enclosing people within their territory. This was also true before the Internet, as people were generally allowed to exit from the territories, but now with the

Internet, an individual does not need to exit from a territory to escape from it. Moreover, the Internet gives him simultaneous access to many territories. It has become easier now for Individuals to access, for example, some information censored in their own countries. They can compare and choose in a manner that is inconceivable in a world of "territorial captivity".

4. 2: Lack of territoriality and disarray of authorities

Governments which attempt to behave in the Internet as they do in the material world quickly find themselves in great disarray. When they forget the immaterial dimension of the Internet, they become unconscious of its specific functioning and they find themselves in difficulties. Failures of attempts by states to regulate the Internet[67] have contributed to the rejection by the Internet users of any legal intrusion. Hence, in order to gain credibility governments should better understand the specific functioning of an immaterial world such as the Internet. This functioning is quite different from the traditional and materialistic world upon which the traditional legal systems are based. A sound understanding of this difference is the condition for a more appropriate State action with regard to the Internet. In the following chapter we shall underline the fundamental difference between the traditional world and cyberspace. This difference is based upon the fact that wealth stems from diverse origins. The traditional world and its legal system are based upon physical economic wealth while in the Internet the origin of economic wealth is the creativity of people, immaterial by essence.

Anna Mancini

CHAPTER 2

WEALTH FROM MATTER AND WEALTH FROM PEOPLE

Positive legal systems, being based upon the concept of territory, give the first place to tangible wealth as well as to the subjective right of property which it naturally involves. A Danish professor of law has criticized our too strong attraction towards material things, as follows:

> The ideas of economists and legal thinkers as well as of those engaged in the social conflicts revolve equally and solely around the external tangible goods, the economic values.[70]

As early as 1929, a long time before the emergence of the Internet, he foresaw that economy would shift from tangible wealth towards immaterial wealth and wrote that intellectual goods would be: "those which future man will look upon as the greatest of values."[71] According to the author, a boom in economic wealth would result from intangible human activities. He already wrote regarding the rights related to people's inventiveness:[72]

> Only a century ago all these rights were, generally speaking, of insignificant practical importance, but in modern times not only the extensive work of legislation in this sphere which has gradually been carried into practice in most countries but also the records of the law courts testify to the crucial importance which these rights have gained in practical business.[73]

Nevertheless, the author could not escape the age-old tradition which granted the first place to the right of property. Hence he proposed to extend the right of property, normally dedicated to tangible objects, to intangible objects such as author's rights, inventions, etc...[74] Despite his visionary analysis of present economic trends, he could not escape the materialistic influence of his time (still existing now) and he focused his study on the right of property, ignoring to a very large extent the category of subjective "personal rights".[75] The continental category of "personal rights" (droits personnels), also called "obligational rights" (droits obligationnels) is, as will be analyzed more deeply later, better fitted than the right of property to stimulate the development of intangible wealth.

1. An age-old materialistic world

1. 1: Matter, the main economic value

The continental legal system owes a lot to late Roman law. Developed in an agricultural context, late Roman law considered the things necessary to run a farm to be of paramount importance. Within a similar agricultural context,[76] continental lawyers have welcomed the late Roman law. You have only to open the French Civil Code[77] to notice at once that the space allocated to people is much less important than the space dedicated to the rights of property and to material things. Even if the right of contracts forms part of its third book, the Code is mainly focused upon tangible wealth and almost ignores intangible wealth. The first book of the Code, entitled "Des personnes" (On persons), contains 508 articles while the two other books entitled "Des biens et des différentes modifications de la propriété" (On goods and on the diverse modifications of property) and "Des différentes manières dont on acquiert la propriété" (on the different ways to acquire the property) total 1768 articles.[78] This clearly demonstrates how much the French Civil Code is the heritage of a mainly rural economy where land was the main source of wealth. Therefore it is not surprising that in such a context, real estate has become the "king of the goods"[79] and the right of property, the king of the subjective rights to the detriment of the category of personal rights. But today, economic wealth is no longer agricultural. It stems more and more from the intangible activities of persons. Hence, we should rather explore the legal category of personal rights, which is better fitted than material rights to the context of the Internet where persons matter. Indeed, intellectual inventiveness and communication skills put the person, and not the matter, at the first place within the Internet. There, we deal with an intangible world and the legal system has to take this fact more into account in order to be effective.

1. 2: Real estate, the king of the traditional economic values

In an economic world initially based upon agriculture, real estate is the most valuable good and therefore the first concern of legal protection. This is so true that we shall see how the legal systems have become obsessed by these goods. The example of French law is very striking. French law gives such importance to real estate that it has gradually assimilated movable things to immovable goods in order to give them the same strong legal status as the one afforded to real estate. In the second book of the Civil Code, related to "Des biens et des différentes modifications de la propriété" (On goods and on the diverse modifications of property) we can read in the article 516: "Tous les biens sont meubles ou immeubles" (Every good is movable or immovable). The simple observation of reality makes obvious the distinction between movable and immovable things, as movable things can be moved while immovable cannot.[80] Nevertheless this natural observation does not correspond to the statement of the French Civil Code. The Code not only distinguishes between movable and immovable things but also

2 4

intermingles fiction and reality by adding to the distinction of things the distinction of rights bearing on things. Rights bearing on things are then sometimes fictitiously assimilated to immovable things despite their very movable and intangible nature. Moreover, the French Code declares that material things, like furniture or animals, which are naturally movable are legally speaking immovable things. Hence pigeons and rabbits have become things immovable by allocation, as stated in the article 524 of the French Civil Code. We are far from the natural distinction between movable and immovable things. While reading the articles 516 to 536 of the French Civil Code we can perceive that we are no longer dealing with the real world but with legal fictions. In effect, the Code considers many movable goods as immovable goods for economic reasons (this relates most of the time to farms). It also considers a right as an immovable thing when it bears on real estate. But a subjective right is something very abstract and only intangible,[81] hence movable by its own nature. A right does not exist in the natural world, it is a fiction[82] invented in the course of the development of legal systems. And the concept of subjective right did not exist in ancient Roman law.[83] It was invented later. Using these fictions as if they were real things the French Civil Code aimed at the best protection of real estate. We can say that the fictitious legal distinction between movable and immovable goods corresponds to the real distinction between things deemed to be valuable to which law intends to grant the best protection and things deemed without great value and less legally protected. We can notice that the Middle Ages French legal say *res movilis, res vilis (movable things, things of poor value)*[84] was far more direct, clear and true that the present Civil Code. In an agricultural economy, law was nevertheless right when giving the first place to the right of property on tangible things. But this policy is no longer valid in a world where economy is shifting towards services and where inventiveness now tends to become a significant source of economic wealth. An inventive idea can nowadays have much more economic value than real estate. The natural distinction between movable and immovable things already existed in Roman law but it has now become extremely complex, as Michel VILLEY[85] states, and is no longer fitted to the economic reality. Such a complexity comes from the fact that sophisticated modern laws tend to escape more and more from reality to evolve in a world of legal fictions. Flowing from this initial confusion another confusion between material rights and personal rights also exists. The material rights, (like the immovable things) are "cherished" by the law, while personal rights are "avoided". Indeed, in a mainly materialistic economy where tangible things are deemed valuable, it is logical to notice that material rights are more attractive than personal rights, the dynamic of which has never really been understood.[86]

1. 3: A traditional preference toward material rights

Even before the Internet, one could notice the growing economic importance of goods such as: literary and artistic works, any kind of inventions and also software.[87] All these kinds of goods were called "information goods" and were paradoxically protected under property rights. For this purpose lawyers invented a new category of right of property which they named "incorporeal property" or "intellectual property". Within this new category of intellectual property rights we can find the authors' rights and the patent right. Despite a more pragmatic approach made by some economists,[88] who have deduced from their practical observations that intellectual rights cannot be rights of property, lawyers cannot realize it. In fact they can hardly change their mind and observe the reality as they are only supposed to deal with substantive law and to apply it. And when the French Code of Intellectual Property[89] declares in a kind of magical[90] way that intellectual rights are rights of property despite their very personal nature and origin, how can a legal engineer think otherwise? If a positive law declares for example that contrary to the simple reality, the author's right is the most sacred and inviolable right of property, a positivistic lawyer cannot challenge this assertion. It is precisely this positivistic legal mental process that the economists we previously quoted could not understand, as for their part they live in the real economic world and not in an abstract legal system which has now cut lawyers off from reality to a very large extent. Moreover the concept of "intellectual property" is also in operation in some international laws[91]. Nobody in the legal field stresses the necessity to become aware of the adverse effects of this vocabulary and the necessity to consider intellectual rights as personal rights. This is not a matter of academic distinctions, it is a question of legal efficiency. If we have a wrong idea of what we are ruling, we cannot find efficient rules. As the Internet is the world by excellence of personal rights and of the wealth they create, we should be aware of the functioning of this category of rights in order to create efficient and useful rules for the Internet. Contrary to the traditional world focused on matter and on rights of property, the Internet is by its own nature the world of persons and hence of personal rights. For this reason we need to have an approach to the category of personal rights which is much more practical and much less ideological.

2. People at the heart of the Internet legal issues

2. 1: People as the driving force behind the economy

Thanks to the Internet the being becomes an increasing source of economic wealth. For this reason it catches the attention of people and tends to become as valuable as matter has ever been. Such a phenomenon should normally contribute to rebalance our too materialistic societies. Such a shift towards a greater interest concerning persons should also contribute to a better understanding of past civilizations that seemed much more concerned with the inner development of human beings than by men's material belongings. In these societies, often considered to be primitive, virtual reality already existed.

What is a virtual world?

Many people imagine that the virtual world of the Internet is totally new. But upon a closer observation of reality, we must reckon that a virtual world has existed for ever. This virtual reality was well known by ancient civilizations like Rome,[92] Greece, or Egypt. The Internet simply makes more available, thanks to machines, an intangible world composed of human thoughts. The Internet in so doing increases the impact of human thoughts on real life. The virtual world of thoughts has primarily been manifested through speech (the *logos*), then through designs, hieroglyphs, and through the diverse forms of handwriting. The printing of books, the new audio-visual media and now the Internet have permitted the acceleration of the circulation of the human thought and have involved the development of the human brain. In comparison with the book, which is material by its own nature, the Internet has given back to the world of thoughts its initial virtuality. By the same token it has also given back to thoughts the laws inherent to the virtual world, that is to say: ubiquity, facility of changes, unlimited and free multiplication, affluence, no limitations..... By freeing creativity and thought from their traditional material media, the Internet highly increases the possibilities for interpersonal exchanges. Through the Internet, people can manifest their creative intelligence and their personality, as well as their tastes and needs, in a way that has never been so free and so easy. Many traditional obstacles cease to exist within the Internet, and that gives place to unprecedented individual freedom. Thanks to the Internet, a person can communicate with other people in real time or not, in the same geographical area or from one point of the globe to another. On the Internet the constraints related to the physical body and to its location in space and time have vanished. The links created between people through the Internet are more than ever "obligations" in the meaning of primitive Roman law, where obligations simply were links (legal or not) within persons, and invisible by their own nature.[93] Taking into account the fact that these invisible links between persons are going to increase to an unprecedented extent, at a worldwide level, and very often without reference to material goods, one can wonder how legal positive systems (and legal minds) adapted to the material world will be able to face the explosion of immaterial wealth involved by the multiplication of personal rights.

From the traditional rights of the personality (protection

of private life, etc.) to the rights of creativity (authors' rights, patent rights, wrongly considered to be rights of property) all the aspects of the persons are affected by the expansion of the Internet. A quick visit to a news group dedicated to law permits at once to notice the increasing number of people now interested in authors' rights. This branch of law, which a short time ago was restricted to a small number of people, now affects any Internet user. Indeed, Internet users should know its basic principles, because of the ease with which authors' rights can be infringed within the Internet, and also the ease with which an author may be published on the Internet. In addition, the number of economic actors in the media industry has increased with the development of the media market. The communication market is now booming and is considered as one of the most profitable markets of the future. Hence some companies which were until now industry-oriented have redirected their investments in this field. This one is directly linked to wealth stemming from persons and is very promising at a worldwide economic level.[94] The human mind[95] not the body, is the target of this phenomenal production and circulation of data. An affluent economy of immaterial wealth is emerging. Being immaterial, this wealth comes from the persons and is directly concerned by the legal category of personal rights. This category is likely to grow in connection with the increase in immaterial wealth.

The development of the category of personal rights

At the end of the twentieth century we have entered what the economists have called the "communication society". The main feature of this new kind of society is a fundamental increase in the economic value of immaterial things in regard to the economic value of material things, as well as an unprecedented increase in business related to immaterial goods.[96] We need only to mention that "The volume of exchange operations is 50 times higher than the volume of the worldwide commerce of goods and services"[97] to understand that the dynamics of this society of immaterial wealth has nothing to do with the ancient agricultural societies marked by scarcity. Those which gave birth to our legal systems and political infrastructures have had a strong and lasting influence on our mentalities. The fast growing technical progress, combined with a more extended use of a common language, allows a faster, worldwide and cheaper circulation of information. This increased circulation leads to a greater economic value of information. When traded worldwide, through the Internet or through the other existing media, a film can bring to the film producer, to the actors, musicians, etc... considerable incomes. The "multimillionaires" of the Internet are not the hardware manufacturers but rather creators of software, those who for example have invented software used all over the world or permitting a high number of visits to specific web sites.[98] The intangible, i.e.; the human creativity consisting in films, software, games, books, pictures or inventions has become an increasing source of economic wealth. It has now become more interesting for large companies to direct their investments toward the immaterial field of economy (media, telephone, the Internet) than toward the traditional material activities. The immaterial field of economy is becoming more profitable and above all more promising than the activities of the past. Despite the close link existing between the expansion of these new markets and the technical devices permitting a higher circulation of information, it is nevertheless the creative intelligence that produces the most significant profits. We can notice that even if matter and immaterial are intermingled, creativity nevertheless is more and more dematerialized. Being more and more dematerialized, creativity frees itself from the constraints of both time and space and can therefore circulate much faster. Meanwhile these constraints which still exist in the traditional world continue to impede the expansion of wealth linked to the dissemination of information under the traditional way. As the Internet puts persons in the fore of the creation of economic wealth, it invites us to reconsider the concept of person and to gain a better understanding of the functioning and *raison d'être* of the legal category of personal rights also called "obligational rights".

2. 2: The concept of "person" through philosophy of law

The word "person" comes from the Latin *persona* and scholars are almost unanimous in admitting that *persona*[99] means "mask", though there is dissent as to whether *persona* means "mask through which one resonates". Many scholars reckon, as Marcel MAUSS did, that the opinion of the Latin etymologist who translated *persona* by "mask through which one resonates" (*per/sonare*) is wrong.[100] Taking into account the translation of *persona* by simple "mask", Jean-Marc TRIGEAUD believes that a slow evolution of the concept of *persona* has taken place towards the Christian concept of person.[101] In the same range of ideas, Stamatios TZITZIS considers the Christian concept of person to be a concept superior to the Greek concept of *anthropos*. In his recent work entitled *Qu'est-ce que la Personne?*, (What is a person?) he explains how in Greece, in the pre-Socratic era, man considered himself as a part of the cosmos and of nature but had not yet reached this degree of recognition of the human personality as a part of the divine, manifested through a physical body, as is the case within Christianity.[102] But, if we make a more serious analysis of ancient Roman law and if we take into account the initial distinction the Romans operated between *actio in rem* and *actio in personam*, the person appears far from being a simple "mask". It is actually a "mask through which one resonates".[103] In the primitive Roman world, the person seems far from being limited to a simple legal role, to a simple mask. Even if the concept of person has not the same spiritual beauty and the same individuality as the one taking place in Christianity, *persona* does not only mean "mask" but above all mask "**through which one resonates**". Such a concept of *persona* gives place to the human self, to the mind, and to the life that flows through the mask. Such an approach to the concept of *persona* modifies the whole perspective. In effect, choosing such a definition of the *persona* and not viewing the *persona* as a play character makes it possible to understand that it is through the body that the person resonates. It is also through the body that a person is influenced by the external world and also through the body that a person can influence the external world. These two last observations are of paramount importance in the field of legal procedures. We believe that the *persona* was the eternal bridge between the tangible and the intangible dimensions of life. The human body is the place where these two sides of reality overlap. This is well illustrated by the works of the ethnologist Claude LEVI-STRAUSS regarding the use of masks in North and South American tribes. He explained that masks were above all means of manifestations of powers (for example healing powers)[104] and means of communication with the dead ancestors. Even though Claude LEVI-STRAUSS mentions the very characteristic example of tribes where buying a mask allows access to a social status,[105] the mask has no value as a simple object, its value is a spiritual one. To these tribes, a mask is a privileged magic means[106] of communication between the visible and the invisible worlds. In ancient Egypt, now more and more recognized as the cradle of the Greco-Roman world this function of "mask through which one resonates" is attested by many practices. They range from the use of statues as intermediary between the divine and the human, to the mummification of the body of the dead which would permit them to communicate with the living through their mummified (and masked) body. Statues as well as mummified human bodies are regarded as life containers.[107] Gods, regarded as point of emergence of cosmic energy, can manifest their power through statues. We did not need to wait for the Christian era, contrary to the belief of Jean-Marc TRIGEAUD, to notice the existence of the idea of the salvation of the individuals' souls. This idea already existed a long time ago in Egypt. As soon as the year 2000 before Christ, Egyptian civilization, long before the birth of the Christian religion, gives a place to the salvation of the individuals' souls, as Joseph SARRAF claims.[108] Far from being limited to a simple "mask", that is to say to his physical body, the human being is something alive, with a life force flowing through the body or "mask". It is on the basis of this very earthly reality that Stamatios TZITZIS writes the following regarding criminal law:

Therefore the body appears to be the foundation of the person; it is through the body that the personality is manifested. Even though we do not mention it and even though it seems to be absent, the body is implicitly present. This fact is obvious within the Criminal Code. Its second book is dedicated to crimes and offences against the persons. Especially, its second part refers to the 'attempts to the human being'. Surely, the human being means for the law a physical dimension and also a psychological one. But the principle of life, prior to express a state of *animus* flows through the body. Hence, when the legislator gives a definition of crime, he primarily aims at the body. Attempts on the human life regard much more aggression against the body than aggression against the soul. For the law, which ignores incorporeal thought, it is the body that can be suppressed and not the soul.[109]

This reality has been perceived a long time ago by the "pre-axial"[110] civilizations. "Pre-axial" was the name given by the philosopher Karl JASPERS to name the civilization marked by myths and magic, having existed before the axial era where Men began rejecting myths and magic and developed their rational minds. In the following part we are going to study, through the theories of the distinction between real (material) rights and personal rights, how the modern world did not pay enough attention to this kind of reality (chapter 1) and widely ignored it. In the second chapter, we shall study how the ancient Roman lawyers used this natural law within the legal field. Then we shall

Anna Mancini

apply their legal knowledge to the Internet.

PART 2

THE LEGAL IMPACT
ON THE VIRTUAL WORLD

THE EXAMPLE OF ANCIENT ROMAN
LAW

In the first part we saw how much the traditional legal world is focused on material wealth, while in cyberspace wealth comes from human beings and not from matter. This kind of intangible wealth nevertheless produces effects on the material world. For this last reason some authors argue that positive laws should apply directly to the Internet, the virtuality of which they deny. They claim that the Internet is not a virtual world, in that it is directed toward people and produces effects on the physical world.[111] But whenever they attempt ruling the Internet with positive laws conceived for a real world -existing in a territory on which states can exert a physical power- they are faced with legal inefficiency. Even if these lawyers are not totally wrong in their approach to the Internet, they simply make the great mistake of not paying enough attention to the fact that there is a connection and an interaction between the physical and the virtual worlds. Actually, matter and virtuality overlap and we cannot ignore this reality. If we want to be efficient lawyers within the Internet we must know what is the "legal translation" of such an overlap. Unfortunately, we cannot find the answer in modern positive laws and the positivistic philosophy of law is irrelevant. Hence if we want to understand what are the effects on the legal architecture of the natural law of overlap between matter and virtuality, we must search for some help in past civilizations which took in account such a phenomenon. The Ancient Roman lawyers did so. They drew benefit from this natural law and invented a legal system that has proved to be very valuable and efficient until now. We can still profitably use their legal inventiveness for the Internet. Regarding pre-axial[112] civilizations, to which the archaic Romans belong, we must rely on archeology and also on knowledge that has reached us in a distorted and misunderstood way. We do not live in the same mental world as the one which gave birth to primitive Roman law. Hence it is not surprising that our way of rational thinking, totally opposed to the primitive way of thinking, impedes a sound and useful understanding of ancient Roman legal knowledge. Regarding the problem we want to solve, i.e.: "how can lawyers efficiently deal with the virtual world of the Internet?", we can find an answer in ancient Roman law. But as this answer has reached us distorted and misunderstood we have to clarify it in order to be able to use it. Today[113] the very positive legal distinction between material rights and personal rights is the only distorted vestige of the legal application the ancient Romans made of the principle of the overlap between matter and virtuality.[114] This modern distinction between material rights and personal rights appears to be a mistranslation of the Roman initial distinction between *actio in rem* and *actio in personam*. The many modern scholars were unsuccessful in trying to find out the reason for the modern distinction between material and personal rights, because they ignored this mistranslation and the remote origins of the positive distinction. Despite an abundant doctrine[115] and the quality of scholars who have dealt with this topic,[116] nobody could reasonably give a correct answer to this wrong question. Today, in France, despite the high volume of doctrine on this subject,[117] one can hear very little about it in law schools. Upon arrival at the university, students are only taught that there are two main categories of rights, material rights and personal rights and that the difference between them is that the material right is absolute while the personal right is relative.[118] Far from conceiving that this point is the mouse that hides an age-old mountain, students will never question this useless assertion. What can be the usefulness of saying that the difference between these two kinds of rights lies in their absolute or relative nature? From there, why not suppress such a useless and misunderstood distinction? This was the proposal some scholars made. An author,[119] having noticed that:

> The doctrine of the distinction between real rights and obligatory rights (rights *in rem* and rights *in personam*) forms one of the most extraordinary chapters in the history of human error.[120]

proposed to give up such a search and noticed:

> In recent years the doctrine of the distinction between real and obligatory rights has occasioned a dispute as to whether the difference between these types of rights must be sought in the content of the right... or in the real protection or in both relations, but it has not been possible to arrive at any agreement or even obtain

lucidity on this point. And there is no result to arrive at, for all this discussion is quite futile, an unnecessary waste of energy that might be applied to better purposes.[121]

Hans KELSEN criticized the still existing distinction between material rights and personal rights in the following words:

This distinction, important in the systematization of the civil law, is also clearly ideological in character. The objection repeatedly raised against it is that a person's legal control over a thing simply amounts to a certain legal relation of the subject to other subjects... If the distinction of the material legal relation is maintained in spite of this objection, it is clearly because a definition of property as a relation between person and thing disguises the socio-economically decisive function of property....[122]

René DEMOGUE[123] reaches the conclusion that the distinction between material rights and personal rights is a useless scientific distinction. It appears to him to be only a scholarly distinction, used for the sake of helping students understand law.[124]

Today the modern trend is to ignore the reasons for such a distinction.[125] Scholars only content themselves with the obsolete distinction proposed by Marcel PLANIOL. They add to it as many new legal categories as there are new kinds of unclassifiable new objects of rights.[126] If it is true that scholarly disputes on the distinction of rights are a waste of time, this does not mean that the ancient Roman law distinction, from which the modern distinction comes, was useless. The problem is that the scholars' positivistic attitude made them unable to escape the frame of positive law and to question the root of the modern distinction they were dealing with. Unfortunately, they took into consideration only the modern distinction even if, as Marcel PLANIOL wrote, this distinction was a mistranslation[127] of a Roman distinction. Moreover, the very concept of right never existed in ancient Rome. As Michel VILLEY explained, it is a modern and abstract invention.[128] Through going to the source of the distinction, scholars could have find out that the initial Roman distinction was linked to the imperative of law enactment.[129] We shall explain in detail how we understand the Roman distinction more easily if we set it back in its historical context and in the mentality of the pre-axial world that produced it. Moreover it appears far more sensible to base our thinking on ancient Roman law where the distinction comes from, rather than on the distorted modern legal remains of the same distinction. By the same token, it is better not to attempt to understand the primitive Roman distinction through the distorted Roman law literature. Unfortunately, Roman Law scholars have the longstanding habit of imposing on Roman Law our modern mentalities as well as our legal philosophy, which were very unfamiliar to the primitive Roman lawyers.[130] This is so true that one author advised not to open modern books on Roman law if we want to understand the Roman legal language.[131]

Without entering into detail of the many theories on the distinction of rights proposed by scholars, which would prove useless for the purpose of the Internet, we shall present the main theories on the distinctions, then we shall propose a more innovative and practical solution drawn from the ancient Roman law. And finally, we shall apply the solution found, as well as Roman legal knowledge, to the Internet.

CHAPTER 3

THE THEORIES OF THE DISTINCTION BETWEEN
MATERIAL RIGHTS AND PERSONAL RIGHTS

1. The traditional theory

This theory is inspired by the works of the ancient scholar: POTHIER.[132] According to the traditional school, the distinction between material rights and personal rights is based upon the object of the rights. The material right bearing on a thing implies a direct link between a person and a thing, while a personal right bears on a person.[133] The traditional theory has been criticized, especially by Marcel PLANIOL[134] who widely contributed to the dissemination of the new personalistic theory of the distinction between material rights and personal rights.

2. The personalistic theory

Marcel PLANIOL expressed the following criticism of the traditional theory: a right in his opinion cannot bear on a thing, insofar as a right always implies links between persons. Marcel PLANIOL noticed that in reality, the right of property cannot be conceived as a direct link between a person and a thing. This direct link is not a right of property. It is simply called "possession". Therefore, according to him the distinction between material rights and personal rights cannot be found on the level of the object of these rights. Any right, real or personal, always implies relations between people. Any kind of right is an obligational right, the difference only exists regarding the number of persons involved in the relationship. Marcel PLANIOL then expressed the famous idea according to which: what distinguishes a material right from a personal right is that a material right is absolute (i.e. opposable to everyone) while a personal right is a relative right (opposable only to a specific number of persons). Despite the obsolescence of this statement, shown especially by René DEMOGUE's works, we can still find it in the majority of law books dedicated to students.[135] René DEMOGUE begins the same way as Marcel PLANIOL, but he reckons nevertheless, that the true distinction cannot lie upon the difference between absolute/relative right as a right is both absolute and relative. The only valid distinction he believes we can operate is between strong rights and weak rights; insofar as there are no technical reasons to establish a distinction between material rights and personal rights.[136]

Opposite to the "personalistic theory" a "realistic theory" has been proposed. The holders of the realistic theory tried to prove that all the rights (material as well as personal) belong to the category of material rights.

3. The realistic theories

The holders[137] of this doctrine envisage all the rights under the category of material rights. One author even uses the personalistic theory (i.e. difference between absolute and relative rights) to prove that all the rights belong to the category of material rights.[138] To arrive at the realistic theory, an author like Vinding KRUSE uses the current analysis of the structure of the subjective rights. Such a structure has been well demonstrated by Edmond PICARD,[139] from which the figures below are adapted.[140] According to the common legal opinion, any subjective right implies the existence of a subject of the right, an object of the right and a content of the right. Edmond PICARD presented as follows the common analysis of the structure of a subjective right:

Edmond PICARD's diagram of a subjective right (n°1)[141]

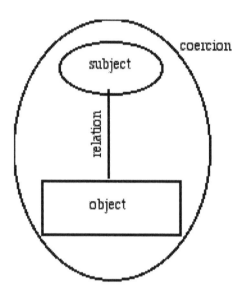

The right of property, a typical material right, is the starting point of the realistic theory invented by Vinding KRUSE.[142] The author has a very intellectual and abstract interpretation of what is a material right. Considering the above structure of rights, he notices that the content of a right of property is notably the power to use, abuse, or enjoy. The content of the right of property is to him a set of prerogatives.[143]

Diagram of the structure of a right of property according to the ideas of Vinding KRUSE (2):

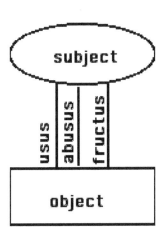

After having analyzed the content of a right of property, the author notices that the same content can apply not only to material things but also to immaterial things such as innovative ideas or literary works. The set of powers does not vary, only the objects do.[144] Hence he deduces that we should extend the traditional way we use the right of property. This right should now apply not only to tangible things but also to any kind of intangible things and to any immaterial goods coming from people's creativity. Vinding KRUSE's proposal for the right of property can be schematized as follows (diagram n°3):

Diagram (3): extended right of property according to Vinding KRUSE

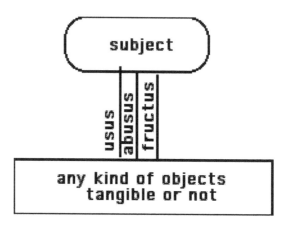

According to the author there is therefore no need to distinguish between material rights and personal rights, insofar as all the rights belong to the category of material rights. Vinding KRUSE's theory was well fitted to the philosophy of positive law which mainly focused on the right of property and on the share of matter. In some aspects, this theory can be compared with the theory of incorporeal property which is also based upon the analysis of the structure of the subjective right of property.[145] The very abstract theories like the theory of incorporeal property, of intellectual property,[146] of the rights on immaterial goods,[147] of intellectual rights or of rights on custom,[148] were all based upon the analysis of the structure of the subjective right. The high amount of scholarly writings dedicated to the distinction resembles the results a computer could render through combining the element of the abstract structure of rights. Hence it is not surprising that these complex abstract and useless theories could never lead to the sound understanding of the initial practical Roman distinction. The primitive Romans did not know the modern concept of subjective rights, which is a very abstract concept. They only dealt with the physical reality and observed the functioning of nature which human beings are part of. As it was based upon a law of physics, the example of the structuring of the legal impact on virtual reality by primitive Roman lawyers is still valid today. We just need to rediscover, through the knowledge that has reached us, the reason why the primitive Romans made a distinction between the *actio in rem* and the *actio in personam*. It is obvious, as we already explained, that if we want to understand the Roman distinction, we must not think on the basis of the mistranslated distinction existing in our modern positive laws. We must forget the idea of subjective rights and its structuring around subject, object and content. This would be a very abstract attitude directly in opposition to the ancient Romans' pragmatic mind. It is with their pragmatic mind, and their taste for the observation of natural phenomena, that Romans built their legal system, so valuable until today.[149] An author stated that Roman lawyers describe realities instead of building ideological systems.[150] We must definitely give up the modern concept of subjective right which has nothing to do in the frame of ancient Roman law. We must stop imposing our modern concepts on past societies. The idea of subjective -personal or real- right, implies the necessary existence of a set of positive laws. Such a set did not exist at the root, when the first Roman lawyers had to invent all from scratch. The first Roman lawyers could not be positivistic lawyers as they had no positive laws to deal with. Their sole option was to observe the real world, to understand it better in order to be able to balance it. Instead of living like modern lawyers in a world of "pure law", of legal classifications and of many useless scholarly distinctions, they were obliged to confront themselves with the "pure reality" of the physical world (including the human beings). Above all, their concern was efficiency in the rendering of justice and not legal theorizing.

CHAPTER 4

THE ROMAN ROOT: THE DISTINCTION BETWEEN *ACTIO IN REM* AND *ACTIO IN PERSONAM*

Being imaginative and practical will help us understand the first Roman lawyers. Let us just try to imagine we are in Ancient Rome and we have to invent law *ex nihilo* as there is no existing set of substantive laws. Firstly, we should remember that if the Roman Law system is still useful today to many different countries it is certainly because it was based not upon a vanishing positive law, but upon an enduring principle. Law aims at improving human life, hence the first thing to do is to observe the world closely. Observing it we can notice that there exist things we can touch, that is to say: material things like stones, plants, animals, and human beings. We can also notice that some "things" cannot be touched but only perceived through the senses and our mind. Such things, consisting of ideas, promises, agreements, obligations, are essential to a legal system. Nevertheless, as well as energy, feelings and the human mind, they pertain to the intangible dimension of life or the immaterial world. We can also notice that a person is both material (through the body) and immaterial (through the mind). A person being both material and immaterial can perceive the intangible world of ideas or agreements, relationships, promises and liabilities as well as the physical world. We can then schematically present as follows these initial observations (diagram n°4):

Diagram (4): observation of the world

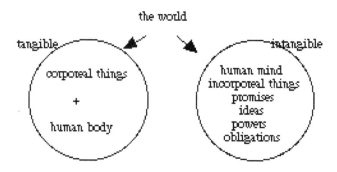

We are able, in a second step, to draw a more accurate diagram (n° 5) because we observe that the human being, through the body and the mind, participates in both the world material and the world immaterial.

Diagram (5): more accurate observation of the world

The world

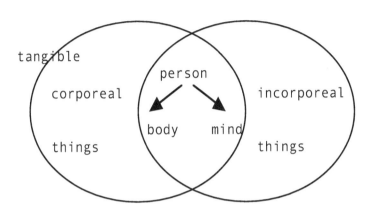

Hence a person appears to be a "bridge" between the material and immaterial dimensions of earthly life. This physico-psychical dimension of human beings was noticed by philosophers like Sören KIERKEGAARD or Immanuel KANT. According to Sören KIERKEGAARD: "Man is a synthesis of the soulish and the bodily".[151] Immanuel KANT invented his concept of "personal right of a real kind" to capture this reality. He writes:

From the fact of personality in the children....Hence the right of the parents is not a purely real right, and it is not alienable (*jus personalissimum*). But neither is it a merely personal right; it is a personal right of a real kind, that is, a personal right that is constituted and exercised after the manner of a real right. It is therefore evident that the title of a personal right of a real kind must necessarily be added, in the science of right, to the titles of real right and personal right, the division of rights into these two being not complete. For, if the right of the parents to the children were treated as if it were merely a real right to a part of what belongs to their house, they could not found only upon the duty of the children to return to them in claiming them when they run away, but they would be then entitled to seize them and impound them like things or runaway cattle.[152]

As persons and their links with the world are at the heart of law, let us observe how people live and which actions are available to them. A person can act upon material things and upon other persons, by physical actions (they can touch them, seize them and move them): this is a natural power of human beings. Regarding the immaterial world, at first sight we could conceive it is impossible to exert a power on it. Upon a closer observation of persons, we realized that we can "act" on the immaterial world by functioning as a bridge between the tangible and the intangible. For example, through the body, a person can perceive an idea, change it, or transmit it to somebody else, who receives it thanks to his own body. In other words, as a person is a bridge between the material and immaterial world, an "action" upon the immaterial world can be effected through persons. For the legal world, in the case of a promise, we can notice that to

obtain the performance of a promise, a person cannot directly act on the promise (take it, touch it, seize it). It is only possible to act upon an individual to make him perform his promise. Hence, an individual may act on immaterial things, always through his own body or the body of someone else. In conclusion, in the context of a legal system, a person can accomplish:
- actions on material things (human body included);
- actions on persons (on persons' mind).

The first Roman Lawyers' aim was to balance the relation between people as well as their powers. When faced with a conflict of powers, Justices had to determine the appropriate power of each litigant. The ancient Roman lawyers distinguished between the *actio in rem* and the *actio in personam* because, on a practical point of view, the power on tangible things is very different from the power on intangible things. By the *actio in rem* a litigant asked a Roman justice: "what is my power on a material thing?" By the *actio in personam* a litigant asked a Roman justice: "what is my power on persons to affect the intangible world?" Now we come to this diagram (n° 6):

Diagram (6): *actio in rem* and *actio in personam*

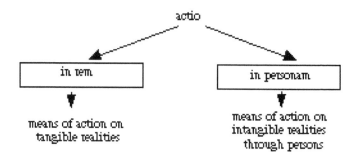

And the solution is: The Roman distinction between *actio in rem* and *actio in personam* is drawn from nature, which allows direct action on material things (*actio in rem*) and only indirect action on the immaterial world through persons (*actio in personam*). There is a simple equation between natural phenomena and legal measures of execution as well as a practical common sense.

We can now schematically present in the two following figures the human powers outside the context of a legal system and the same powers in the context of the Roman legal system:[153]

Diagram (7): human powers outside the context of a legal system

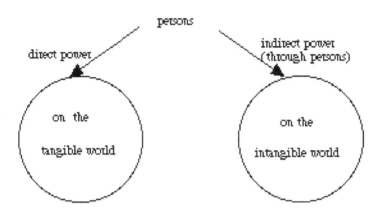

Diagram (8): powers within the context of the Roman legal system

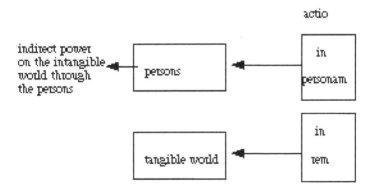

When a person had an *actio in rem,* a justice determined his power on a tangible thing. When a person had an *actio in personam* a justice decided what power, to be exerted upon other persons, this person had on an intangible thing.

The second diagram widely corresponds to Justinian's distinction between persons, things and actions. MICHAS underlined the influence of Justinian's distinction on the continental legal systems, especially the distinction between things, persons and actions.[154] It suffices, however, to realize that the real world being unchanged, a classification based upon nature will last for ever. The Roman distinction between *actio in rem* and *actio in personam* stems from a natural law: the overlap between the material and immaterial dimension of earthly life. It is because this distinction is based upon nature and not upon the positive law of a given past society that it is still valid and useful to any kind of societies. The basic Roman distinction was mistranslated within the continental legal systems where it became the distinction between material right (droit réel) and personal right (droit personnel). The concept of right which does not pertain to physical natural laws is an abstract legal concept ancient Romans ignored. Using such a modern concept prevented modern scholars from finding, in the context of substantive law, the reason for such a mistranslated distinction.

The basic Roman distinction between *actio in rem* and *actio in personam* is related to the fact that so-called primitive civilizations were, as their interest in myths, magic, astrology or divination proves, much more familiar than us with the immaterial dimension of life we tend to neglect.

With their pragmatic approach to life, the first Roman "lawyers" took into account the physical realities and drew from them appropriate legal procedures. To act upon the tangible world they did as we do, they acted directly upon material things, whereas regarding the immaterial world they were more practical than we are. With good common sense they understood that upon Earth, action on the virtual dimension of life can only be effected through a physical body. They observed that by the body, a human being is a bridge between the two dimensions of life. Hence, in order to act upon the invisible world it is enough to act through a human being. On a procedural ground, these practical views gave place to the invention of the *actio in personam*, which wording clearly shows that it consists in acting **inside** a person and not **on** the body. The distinction between the two material and immaterial dimensions of our world is highly useful to our modern legal world where more and more legal questions relating to the immaterial dimension are raised. If we pay more attention to the ancient Roman legal vocabulary, say ligare (to *bind*) or deligare (to *unbind*), we become well aware of the interest of the ancient civilizations in the intangible side of the human life made of many intangible bonds or links between persons.[155] Today we still use the same measures of execution as in ancient Rome. We have found no means of actions on intangibles which differ from action on persons. Consequently and as an example, if someone "steals" an invention, the injured person never claims for the return of the inventive idea, but instead asks for an injunction against the counterfeiter to cease producing the invention. This is in fact an *actio in personam* and not an *actio in rem* and the concept of property generally applied to the field of patent law is thoroughly irrelevant. Despite the success of the concept of incorporeal property applied to inventions or literary works, criminal law conflicts with the idea of stealing immaterial things like innovative ideas. In the context of criminal law, a theft implies the mastery of the stolen thing by the thief and the victim's aim is to recover the thing. So, in the context of industrial property for example, it is easy to observe the impossibility to steal an inventive idea and to recover it because we cannot touch it. Patent law does not apply sanctions against a theft, but against the unauthorized working of an inventive idea. It uses an action for infringement of patent directed against persons but never against ideas.[156]

CHAPTER 5

TESTING THE FINDINGS

1. Through the ancient Romans' practical sense

Scholars unanimously recognize that the ancient Romans were very practical. This is underlined by Pierre GRIMAL throughout his book entitled *La civilization romaine*[157] and also by MICHAS,[158] and by Van BEMMELEN.[159] Samuel GINOSSAR also comments on the Roman legal instinct.[160] As for Michel VILLEY, he particularly confirms the validity of such a process. He has demonstrated through many examples how the Romans observed the nature of things.[161] He also underlined that to Romans nature meant all that exists, including the body and mind of human beings.[162] VILLEY also affirms in a study on legal reasoning that Roman lawyers did not proceed as "scientifically"[163] (logically) as we do. Being practical people, the ancient Romans did not build a fictitious and abstract legal system. They granted only natural actual powers. They would not for example grant a direct mastery[164] over an intangible thing, as that is practically impossible. If the Romans, from their standpoint, heard us discussing "intellectual property" or "intangible property" they would probably laugh at us, and certainly believe that we are "under developed" persons.

Relating to the observation of nature in Roman Law, Michel VILLEY quotes many examples showing that all legal acts, agreements, etc., that were impossible to perform because contrary to nature, were void and null in Rome. In other words, what nature does not allow cannot be allowed by human will.[165] VILLEY gave the example of a testimony containing provisions void as contrary to nature. The author also quotes another text about the necessary nullity of a judgment contrary to the nature of things.[166]

2. Through the concept of property

In various studies, we encountered the idea that property is a fact. We can read in JUSTINIAN's Institutes that property is "*plena in re potestas*" (full power on a thing).[167] Roman people never claimed an abstract right of property before a tribunal; they directly asked for the thing by saying "*rem meam esse*" (this is my thing).[168] In fact, it is more natural and pragmatic to ask directly for the thing instead of asking for a "right". The modern and abstract concept of right was ignored by the natural and pragmatic primitive Romans. The idea that property implies mastery over physical things clearly appears in POTHIER's writings concerning the concept of property.[169] This idea is still naturally expressed by modern legal scholars like Stamatios TZITZIS who writes: "The respect of property is at the heart of law. We can only master what we possess".[170]

3. Through the Egyptian origins of ancient Roman Law

The rebirth of the study of ancient Roman Law took place long before Jean-François CHAMPOLLION deciphered the Egyptian hieroglyphs and in so doing opened the doors of Egyptian thought. It is only recently that more and more Egyptologists and Historians have began to underline the obvious link between the Greco-Roman world, which shaped our axial age, and ancient Egypt.[171] Due to this fact, the link between ancient Roman Law and the ancient Egyptian civilization is seldom referred to. Roman Law scholars remain confined to their specialty and show no interest in Egyptology which is another specialty.[172] As for Egyptologists, they show no interest in Roman law, which would be of great help if linked with Egyptology. As early as 1912, Eugène REVILLOUT demonstrated how much Rome has drawn from Egypt, through the study of the legal institutions of the late Roman period. His book, entitled *Les origines égyptiennes du droit civil romain*[173] (on the Egyptian origins of Roman Civil law), remained isolated and widely ignored.[174] This work is interesting and convincing but restricted to the study of civil law concepts like *mancipatio* or *fiducie* from the late Roman period. It does not address the philosophy which gave birth to this legal system. It is useful for our purpose to go to the philosophical roots, as they show the common features between ancient Roman law and Egyptian culture, more obviously than the study of the institutions of the late period.[175] Through this common ground, we become better able to understand for example the origin and the meaning of the Roman concept of *persona*, which becomes a further proof of the reason why the Romans made a distinction between the *actio in rem* and *actio in personam*. We are now going to explain these common features. Here, We do not detail everything that regards Egypt as we shall study it in more depth in the part dedicated to the idea of justice in ancient Egypt.

3. 1: A strong practical sense, common to Romans and Egyptians

Both the ancient Egyptians and the ancient Romans were practical people.[176] Their method of work was not scientific in the modern way and they had a clear preference for symbolic communication. In an interesting book on Roman Law, Michel VILLEY has shown how the ancient Romans' law stemmed from the practice and the observation of life. They had no *a priori* definitions (for example of personality, of property), but only practical solutions to daily life questions. Roman law was not a system but the art of finding what is fair and according to Michel VILLEY, the art of sharing.[177] As archeology has revealed, the ancient Egyptians were also very practical and above all clever observers of nature.[178] In the frame of his translation of the moral Papyrus of Boulaq, Emile AMÉLINEAU[179] explained how much the Egyptians were practical even in the field of morality. He came to use the word "utilitarian" to qualify their approach to morals. In addition we know that the ancient Egyptians were very interested in the origins of the world, and that they also applied their practical sense to this quest, as was underlined by the Egyptologist L. GOFF:

...they were essentially practical, not philosophical people. When they considered what was really a philosophical question, such as the origin of the world and life as they knew it, it was because this question had a bearing on some problem they had to face...[180]

3.2: The creative power of the spoken word and the concept of *persona*

Contrary to our modern world, which is mainly logical, materialistic and -we have to admit it- self-important, so-called primitive civilizations like Rome, Greece or Egypt were much more interested in persons than we are. Through ancient Roman law and through the Egyptian concept of justice we can see how these peoples used within the legal field the natural law of the overlap between material and immaterial realities, a reality that our legal systems ignore. Thanks to their pragmatism, the ancient Egyptians and the ancient Romans paid attention and drew benefit from a natural law that the modern world has applied only recently in the field of Information technology. This natural law simply consists of the fact that there is a constant interaction between material and immaterial, which involves the manifestation of the intangible through tangible things. It is this same principle, the passage or the obstruction of an energy through a physical thing, which is applied to information technology and thanks to which the Internet exists. We can find an application of this same principle in ancient Egypt through the approach to creative speech and through rituals. The ancient Romans too used this principle in their concept of *persona*, without which the ancient Roman distinction between *actio in rem* and *actio in personam* would never have existed. The Egyptian world is strongly marked by the importance given to speech. Which according to Egyptian literature was a living and creative substance received through the hearts of humans and of gods and emitted by the tongue. This Egyptian philosophy, which we shall explain more in detail in the next chapter, is obviously close to the role played in ancient Roman law by the legal spells.[181] For example, in primitive Roman law, where the concept of **right of** property was unknown, whenever somebody wanted to claim before the judges what we would call today "a right of property" say on a land, the claimant had to use a ritualistic spell by which he declared that the land was his own land. He had to act in the formalistic way prescribed, that is to say he had to pronounce the exact spell the judge previously granted him. According to the case, the claimant had to bring a clod of earth or any object in connection with the thing claimed. This, finally is similar to magical rituals.[182] The spells of the Law must be spoken in their exact words, or no judgment would be possible. Originally these spells were kept secret by the pontiffs (ancient Roman kind of priest). It is only much later that the spells began to be written and later on published.[183] By reciting a spell of the law before a Pontiff the ancient Romans used the same principle as Egyptian people: the principle of "voice emission". The "emission of voice" is a creative act which on a technical standpoint consists in letting the sound pass through a material thing: the physical body. Hence the Roman concept of *persona* is actually in conformity with the etymology *per-sonare* which means the mask through which one resonates. In other words the *persona* is a physical vector allowing the passage of intangible things like life and voice (to which the Ancient Egyptians paid special attention). Such a view obviously constitutes the fundamental ground of the distinction between *actio in rem* and *actio in personam*. In fact, if the physical body of persons allows the manifestation of the intangible (say ideas), it is easy to such practical people to verify the fact that it is also through the

71

body of persons (by a physical act or by words) that it is possible to act on the intangible. The ancient Roman distinction, between *actio in rem* and *actio in personam*, is one of the practical applications of the law of interaction between matter and immaterial in the human body. As, in substance, Roman Law was built upon nature and not upon political and social foundations, it has lasted. Many countries have been able to benefit from it[184] and today we can even draw a remarkable profit from it in the field of the Internet. Let us now apply the ancient Roman knowledge to the Internet.

CHAPTER 6

ROMAN KNOWLEDGE APPLIED TO THE INTERNET

The Roman distinction between *actio in rem* and *actio in personam* can be usefully applied to the Internet. It brings light on the right way to approach the Internet. In fact, there is a contradiction among those who uphold the virtual nature of the Internet and those who oppose it. When, commonly, some speak about the virtual world, cyberspace, some lawyers answer that the Internet does not involve a virtual world. To them, the Internet should be submitted to substantive law insofar as it products its effects on the real world and regarding real people. Hence their wish to rule the Internet with traditional legal systems and the impasse to which they lead. In so doing, they apply the positivistic logic we are now going to present.

1. The positivistic legal process facing abuses in cyberspace

1°) Lawyers notice there are some abuses committed in the

Internet.

2°) They want to punish such abuses and to forbid them.

3°) They esteem there is no legal gap[185] insofar as positive law should be applied to the Internet which is not a virtual world but a real world dealing with real people and producing some effects on the material world.

4°) They ask themselves which law should apply. Unfortunately so many laws from so many countries can be applied[186] that it is very hard to make a decision.

5°) While they assert that the Internet is not "a purely virtual world", that there is no legal gap, and that the existing law should naturally apply to the Internet, lawyers nevertheless publish many books entitled say "Internet law" or "Cyberspace law".[187] Some countries have passed laws specific to the Internet or are intending to do so.

6°) All the lawyers notice that, due to the importance of the territoriality criterion in the traditional law, it is hard to apply the traditional law within the Internet where this criterion is irrelevant. Today a State cannot use the commodity of its territory and of its physical borders to forbid, say, dissemination or access to undesirable information.[188] This has become impossible, as we shall study more in depth with the example of the *American Communications Decency Act*. Through the brief summary of the reasoning lawyers use to attempt solving the problems raised by the Internet we can notice how much this logic is only seeming and how much lawyers and governments are in an impasse. Such a positivistic approach to the Internet does not take into account the dynamics of the Internet and of its ensuing prosperity. It leads only to an inefficient complexity. Ancient Roman law can help improve this situation.

2. The help of ancient Roman law

Ancient Roman law allows us to show the supporters and the opponents of the virtual nature of the Internet that they are both wrong and right. To human beings there exists no virtual world completely severed from the material world. Without a material thing men cannot perceive the intangible world. In fact it is always through matter, whether a human body or a computer for the Internet, that a human being has access to all kinds of "virtual worlds". The current legal confusion and its ensuing inefficiency stem mainly from a lack of observation of the functioning of the Internet with regard to the law of interaction between the tangible and the intangible sides of reality. Being aware of this principle, one just needs to apply the ancient Roman distinction between *actio in rem* and *actio in personam* and the question is clarified. The Roman distinction resulted from the impossibility of acting directly upon the intangible virtual world. This leads to the following practical consequences which should be taken into account on legal grounds. In order to act upon the virtual world of the Internet, we have to do it through "physical things" through which information can flow. That is to say the persons (through the body) and the computers. Hence the broad philosophical outline which should be the fundamental basis of an Internet law, should be the following:

1°) If the Internet is a simple communication tool used by well-identified users in order to trade tangible goods which will be delivered to a clearly and legally identified place, then traditional law can apply and it is not necessary to add new Internet laws for such cases.

2°) If the Internet is used in order to exchange intangible goods (electronic books, services, pictures....). As soon as the people exchanging these goods cannot be physically identified we have no possibility of acting upon the intangible. Hence any kind of legislation trying to do so will fail and be ridiculous. The only way to act upon the intangible is through persons, and in such a case the "person" does not exist from a legal standpoint. In such a case the sole recourse of public authorities consists in influencing the ideas of people by circulating legal recommendations and launching campaigns. That is to say they will act upon people through speech, as the ancient civilizations well understood.

3°) When the Internet is used to exchange intangible things only (which does not have the effect of leading to material exchanges) and the persons involved in the exchange are well legally determined. In case of conflict, the national laws can be applied under two conditions: Firstly there exists a law regarding the infringement; Secondly the conflicting persons are citizens of the same country or when they are not, an International agreement applying to this case exists.

In case of dispute arising:

- in connection with intangible exchanges through the Internet to which International law cannot apply because there is no International agreement dealing with the specific matter involved or because, due to the characteristics of the Internet, the exchange cannot be posited in a given territory and/or some or all of people involved cannot be identified. There exists no possibility for a given State to punish infringements and to balance the conflicting interests on a legal ground.

3. A new application of the Roman law distinction made possible by the Internet

Roman law, as we have explained, helps us understand that, within the Internet, we have to distinguish what is tangible from what is not, in order to conceive an efficient legal action upon the virtual world. Like the ancient Romans, it is still through the persons that we are able to act upon the intangible world. But now there is something new: with the Internet we can also act upon the intangible through computers.[189] In case of a dispute arising within the Internet, at an international level, the legal measures of execution should be exerted, when possible, against persons and in such a case we need "worldwide laws". That is to say laws which do not refer to territories in order to be effective. Measures of execution or of legal prevention can also be exerted through computers by using specific technical tools. This possibility has been studied by authors like Lawrence LESSIG or Mark STEFIK. Thanks to the Ancient Roman expertise we have now a clearer view on how to deal legally with the Internet in an efficient way. But normally, law should be aimed at justice and we cannot apply to the Internet our traditional view of justice.[190] That is to say mainly ARISTOTLE's justice giving to "each his own". Indeed, in a world of information affluence where giving information to someone does not deprive the donor, justice as the art of sharing is nonsense and moreover totally useless. Hence if states can no longer justify their intervention by this kind of justice and if they content themselves with levying tax on the Internet, it is not surprising that States intervention is not welcome. Many Internet users are asking about the legal intervention of states within the Internet: "Is it still justified?"[191] In order to be justified, the legal intervention of states should be based upon an idea of justice suited to the Internet and not on a set of laws which were created in order to share material things. Where can we find an idea of justice which would apply to a virtual world and which would justify legal interventions? Roman law cannot help, nor positive law, nor the classical philosophy of justice. Fortunately, Ancient Egypt can be of great help insofar as this civilization was very much concerned with an idea of justice suited to the intangible.

Let us now present what justice was to the ancient Egyptians.

PART 3

WHICH KIND OF JUSTICE

FOR THE INTERNET?

Anna Mancini

We have already shown that, deprived of an aim of justice, governmental attempts to regulate the Internet are likely to be rejected by the Internet users. A view of primitive Roman law makes it obvious that the idea of justice is a prerequisite to the existence of substantive laws and positive legal systems.[192] The invention of a legal system implies the prerequisite of an interest in rendering justice. No societies exist where the positive law does not derive from an initial will to render justice. This simple statement tends to be forgotten by modern lawyers dealing only with a well established set of laws. Moreover, the positivistic legal theory prevents them from having an interest in justice. Such a lack of interest places our modern legal world in total contradiction with the Egyptian legal world. Indeed, what mattered in Egypt was justice and not law. We find here a striking example of a successful civilization focused on justice but showing no interest in laws and codes. When one realizes that the conflicts raised by the competition between national laws provide the major legal and insoluble problem faced within the Internet, why not try to understand how the Egyptians successfully managed to create a prosperous civilization without a need for codes and laws? Why not follow the example of the Egyptian focus on justice, instead of wasting time with laws that were created for another world?[193] Well, but which kind of justice can suit the Internet? ARISTOTLE's justice which gives "to each his own" and fairly shares material goods existing in a limited number, is no longer useful within the Internet.[194] The same applies to the variations of the Aristotelian theme of justice proposed by many philosophers. Even John RAWLS has built his *Theory of Justice* on this ground, useless for the Internet.[195] As the Aristotelian concept of justice has been prevailing since the dawn of our axial era, lawyers and philosophers can hardly imagine a thoroughly different kind of justice. But ARISTOTLE's justice and its subsequent variations are totally irrelevant when applied to the Internet. Hence we are faced with the necessity of finding another idea of justice, a justice which deals with the intangible world of information rather than with matter. Indeed it is a very difficult challenge as the classical philosophy cannot be of help. Fortunately the study of ancient Egypt itself contains the answer. It is obvious that until now lawyers have ignored the very aim of justice and have focused their attention on the positive law.[196] Governments for their part have generally been driven more by their fear of losing power and tax revenues than by a will to render justice. There is no philosophy justifying governmental or legal action on the Internet and even less a reflection on what a concept of justice suited to the Internet should be. Instead, with a very poor sense of innovation, lawyers worldwide continue to ask for example: Which law should apply? Which court should decide? Is such and such behavior occurring within the Internet punished by a positive law?[197] Insofar as the ancient Egyptians made their concept of justice essential to the creation of immaterial wealth, this concept is a valuable guide for lawyers, governments economists and philosophers in their approach to the Internet. We are now going to present the ancient Egyptian idea of justice, a concept that until now has remained ignored in the field of legal studies.

Anna Mancini

SUB-PART 1

PHILOSOPHY OF JUSTICE

IN ANCIENT EGYPT

CHAPTER 7

ANCIENT EGYPT, A CIVILIZATION FOCUSED ON JUSTICE

The archeological remains of Egyptian civilization clearly prove that justice was essential to this people. Insofar as ancient Egypt was much more interested in justice than in law, it was a world very unlike ours. Egypt did not leave us a legal system as the Ancient Romans did, [198] but rather an idea of justice that our modern mentalities can hardly understand. Purely legal Egyptian archeological remains are very rare: only a few texts from the Late Period have been found. One of them, considered by Egyptologists to be the first international treaty, has reached us. [199] But the topic of justice can be found in the very acts of daily life. Almost all the texts and inscriptions discovered speak of justice. Egyptian justice deals not only with earthly life but also with the afterlife. Though the title of his book *La notion du droit d'après les Anciens Egyptiens* (the idea of law according to the Ancient Egyptians) Joseph SARRAF is also obliged to stress how essential the concept of justice was for this civilization and to highlight the scarcity of purely legal texts. [200] All the texts of wisdom teach that one has to conform to Maat, an unclear concept that Egyptologists have translated into the expression "Goddess of Truth and Justice". Through the ancient Egyptian *Book Of The Dead*, we know that justice is the measure by which the dead will be judged when passing on and coming before the balance of Maat. [201] This passing through the scales is shown in the illustrations called "vignettes" accompanying many funerary texts. As the passing through the balance of Maat appears to be a compulsory step before reaching the afterlife, it is easy to understand to what extent justice was an essential component of this ancient civilization which was so concerned about the afterlife. Therefore, the omnipresence of Maat, the Goddess of Truth and Justice, is not surprising. She appears in almost every text that Egyptologists have translated, such as texts of wisdom, funerary papyri, or hieroglyphic inscriptions carved on temple walls. Information on Maat was collected not only from the translation of texts but also from pictures. Maat is the goddess with the white feather, the one who also holds an Ankh cross (symbol of life) in her hands. Through the remains of Egyptian civilization, we can easily understand that an Egyptian's whole life was governed by Maat. In such a world there is no difference between divine and human justice. The just man on Earth is also just in the afterlife. He is rewarded with lifely affluence, with prosperity in his earthly life as well as in his afterlife. Egypt as a "gift from the Nile" is marked by material prosperity which nevertheless did not stop it from striving for a high ideal of justice. But its concept of justice is so different from ours that the Egyptologists and the Historians of religions find it extremely hard to define it properly. As for modern legal researchers, amongst them there is very little interest in researching into the Egyptian concept of justice, which is generally completely ignored.

As Egyptian justice aimed the creation of immaterial wealth, the understandable interest of lawyers and governments should be to rediscover Egyptian justice in order to apply to the Internet an expertise that marked the longevity as well as the prosperity of the ancient Egyptian civilization.

Anna Mancini

CHAPTER 8

EGYPTIAN JUSTICE AND FREE FLOW OF IDEAS

Jan ASSMANN[202] believes that if we were able to understand the meaning of Maat, we would get a key to understanding the ancient Egyptian world. But this concept is extremely difficult for our modern minds to understand, for the two following reasons:

1°) Eric HORNUNG underlined that in modern languages no word related to law matches Maat,[203] however we ever try to compare Maat, the goddess of justice, with concepts we are used to dealing with in the legal modern world. Scholars reckon that the ancient Egyptians did not pass on to us a clear definition of what Maat is. In fact the Egyptians gave many "Egyptian definitions" of Maat, especially in the rituals of the offering of Maat. The truth that, whenever we try to find in Maat a concept of justice, in accordance with our modern values, we cannot understand the definitions the Egyptians gave of Maat.

2°) A second main reason is that modern world has the intellectual habit of dealing with great problems by dividing them in smaller questions and in many fields of expertise.

This behavior is totally opposite to the Egyptian mind where all the aspects of life and knowledge were integrated.[204] For example, it is impossible to have a sound understanding of the concept of Maat if we study it apart from the Egyptian concept of heart.

This is the reason why, in order to unveil the Egyptian concept of Maat, we are going to select from Egyptian literature the permanent information related to Maat, the sun, the functioning of the human body, and especially to the heart. To do so, we have searched through Egyptian literature for useful information for the understanding of Maat. While a large amount of information on Maat is available, a coherent definition of Maat has never been drawn from it. The main reason, as we already mentioned, is that Maat has been studied apart from elements that were necessary to its sound understanding. Another reason is our weakness for imposing modern concepts onto Egyptian concepts. Along with the presentation of the valuable information we have selected, we shall give the Egyptian sources in the footnotes. The collected information will allow us to answer the following points:
- definition of Maat and of its opposite,
- how the flow of Maat produces positive results,
- how Maat circulates in human society,
- what obstructs the right flow of Maat in human society,
- how Maat allows us to understand the unity of all the spheres of life in Egypt,

- why Maat is not actually justice, though she is, as well as the heart, one of its essential components.

1. What is Maat, and what is its opposite?

Through the texts we know that Maat is a cosmic energy which reaches human beings through the sun,[205] through the gods and also through the Pharaoh. We can even find the definition of Maat in one of Rameses II's names: Usermaatra-Setepenra which means: "Maat is the strength of Ra, the beloved of Ra".[206] This cosmic energy manifested as light[207] or power[208] on the human level is also manifested as happiness, good health, strength, life,[209] prosperity, stability (i.e. horizontality, righteousness,[210] balance) and harmony. A passage from the *Coffin Texts* clearly states that Maat is life.[211] We can also understand Maat through the opposite results of the absence of Maat.[212] Without Maat, there is darkness, chaos, loss of life force, poverty, illness, destruction, death. In the Egyptian language the opposite of Maat is "Isfet".[213] Like the concept of Maat, it is hardly understandable and the many different translations proposed are considered to be approximate by the experts. One among them considers it to be a very unclear word,[214] while Jean YOYOTTE considers that this word can be translated into "chaos".[215] We know through many texts that Maat destroys the enemies of Ra[216] and that darkness is the major enemy of

Ra.[217] Hence if Maat is the light creating life, it is easy to see in Isfet, the darkness involving death. This way we can better understand why in the hieroglyphic writing the drawing of a solar black disk means the non-being[218] and also why Maat should not be offered to the god of war.[219] A passage from a *Hymn To Khnum* considers light to be life.[220] This view of Maat also clarifies the following passage of Ani's *Book Of The Dead*: "Chapter LXXX Spell to make the transformation into god who gives the light in the darkness", where Maat is in Ani's body and where Ani says he is the woman who enlightens the darkness.[221] On a cosmic level, the flow of Maat involves the cosmic balance, where the "stability" of Ra (the sun) in the sky is essential to the ancient Egyptians. Maat is the energy that feeds the whole cosmos. Maat feeds the sun, which also breathes her,[222] she feeds all the gods. This makes more clear one of the hieroglyphic writing of Maat, the plinth ⬛ reminding the basis of things and also horizontality.

2. The law of Maat and its positive results

In order to produce positive results, Maat must flow without obstructions. From there comes the importance, often emphasized by the experts, of the ritual of the offering of Maat to the sun. It is through this ritual that the Pharaoh partakes in the cosmic order, while any human being can do the same with a physical organ: the heart. As for the sun, it makes all the hearts[223] live, it breathes Maat,[224] its energy enters in the hearts[225] while the heart is the root of life of every human being.[226] The heart is omnipresent in the Egyptian literature and many expressions are created from it. The ancient Egyptian listens with the heart,[227] understands with the heart, speaks with the heart, makes a decision with the heart,[228] wants with the heart,[229] is guided in his life by the heart.[230] He lives thanks to the heart,[231] speaks of the heart of the sun and the gods, unites himself to the sun through the heart, unites himself with the heart of his *ba*,[232] has a righteous heart,[233] is under the protection of the heart while sleeping,[234] lives during the day thanks to the energy of the heart. When the heart is tired his members are weak. Sometimes the animal's heart cries.[235] In short, information on the heart is abundant[236] and lets easily understand how Maat flows among people.

3. The flow of Maat among people

We know through many texts that the heart receives Maat from the sun,[237] it picks it up through the hearing[238] and through the senses. In chapter XVIII of Ani's papyrus we can read that Ani has a heart full of Maat.[239] We know by the Prophecies of Neferti that when solar disk is veiled, men are deaf.[240]

The heart is the physical means of the circulation of

energy.[241] The benefit which can be drawn from the law of the flowing or non-flowing of an intangible energy through a tangible body or device which "conveys the power"[242] seems to have been understood by the ancient Egyptians before the age of information technology.[243] If the heart is open to Maat, i.e. if it receives well, if it "hears the cosmic energy well",[244] this is a good thing, but it is not enough to create harmony. The energy must circulate too, i.e. it must be correctly emitted and mainly through the tongue (this means through speech) and through actions (that is to say the behavior as well as the gesture). Hence we can understand why speech was so essential to the ancient Egyptians. And also why, in the legal field, so many civilizations have given so great an importance to the "promise", or to the strict observance of the "spells of the law" (in ancient Roman law for example). The speech is Maat. It is Maat received in the heart,[245] transformed and emitted from the tongue. Hence the speech is solar energy flowing into humanity as a whole. Trough the speech ideas flow among people.

4. The obstacles to the free flow of Maat

The circulation of Maat can be obstructed in many ways. Among these we find especially lies,[246] abhorred by the gods according to the ancient Egyptians. But the word "lie" in Egypt, as we know thanks to many texts, has a very specific and concrete meaning. Above all, it does not refer to any kind of morals. In the Egyptian world, to lie consists in not speaking (and also probably not acting) according to what is felt in the heart, in other words not in compliance with Maat. A liar disturbs the flow of Maat which results in imbalance in himself and around him. The lie is indeed the abhorrence of the gods, as it hinders the correct flow of Maat. The very first victim of the lie is the liar himself. In this very life he will suffer from physical as well as psychical disorders involved by the incorrect flow of energy in him. On the other hand, truth is loved by the ancient Egyptians and has also a very specific and non-moral meaning. To tell the truth means to be fair. One tells the truth when he speaks according to the heart, that is to say according to the correct flow of Maat.[247] Hence speaking the truth means living in compliance with Maat, with the appropriate circulation of energy through the cosmos and through the human society considered as forming part of the cosmos. It is therefore easier to understand the Egyptian expression "fair of voice".[248] It just means that the voice is fair when it is emitted in compliance with the heart, that is to say in compliance with the right flow of Maat. As the *Text Of Memphite Theology*[249] explains, one of the results of such a fair voice is creativity, inventiveness due to the emission of life energy through the voice. Another way to hinder the flow of Maat is "the greed of the heart" the Egyptian condemned[250] so vividly. Nevertheless the greed of the heart, as well as lie or truth, does not involve ethical and moral values. It is not a sin as the modern mind would believe it. To the Egyptians the greed of the heart is only a malfunction[251] of the heart, which can be corrected. A man with a greedy heart is unable to exchange, and to make Maat circulate. He is the first who suffers from this malfunction of the heart; as he does not receive all the good things Maat conveys.[252]

A third way of obstructing the flow of Maat consists in "swallowing the heart" or "eating the heart".[253] We could not find the clear meaning of these expressions within Egyptian literature. They seem to refer to a lack of exchange, something like a "close circuit".

A fourth manner of obstructing the flow of Maat consists in inability to receive it. This occurs mainly when the "hearing" is bad. While the lightness of the heart is a good quality to the modern world, it is a defect to the ancient Egyptian world. To them lightness of the heart was not an abstract and moral concept. Hence having a light heart was far from being a good thing. It meant not having enough Maat in the heart, and in consequence being not sufficiently alive.[254] A text states that the lightness of the heart results in heaviness in bodily gesture.[255] While *a contrario* another text mentions that being full of Maat brings good health.[256]

5. Maat: the link between all the spheres of life

All the human beings are linked together by the circulation of Maat through their hearts. Even the sun has a heart.[257] In consequence, Maat appears naturally to be the reason why, in the ancient Egypt, all the aspects of life - social, political, scientific as well as what we perceive as religious- were united. All was considered under the angle of circulation of Maat as an energy.

The ancient Egyptian world was focused on two main aims depending on the correct circulation of Maat. One was inner well-being: good health, happiness, vitality; the other was external material prosperity.[258] This material prosperity was also closely dependent on the right circulation of Maat.[259] Light and white,[260] Maat is an energy (solar energy, cosmic energy or life force) which must circulate. The Egyptian people were mainly seeking happiness and vitality and the repeated wish addressed to the Pharaoh was: "life -good health- strength". As Claire LALOUETTE explains, this was the abbreviation for the sentence: "May he live, be in good health and prosperous".[261] This sentence was placed after the writing of each royal name.[262] As the modern world lacks interest in the inner prosperity of human beings, we know very little about human energy. The ancient Egyptians applied their knowledge regarding the flow of solar energy in order to create physical wealth successfully. Hence the Egyptian concept of justice constitutes an example of applied philosophy to be profitably used within the Internet which also lets the "speech" circulate. Now, let us define what justice was to the Ancient Egyptians.

6. What is the ancient Egyptian justice?

White and light Maat is not justice, but justice consists in letting Maat flow correctly. To dispense justice is therefore to re-establish the correct circulation of Maat or to impede obstruction to the correct flow of Maat. Finally, the ancient Egyptian concept of justice appears to be very different from our abstract and modern idea of justice. In Egypt, justice was a life process consisting in establishing or re-establishing, through the balance between matter and energy, the correct and harmonious flow of cosmic energy (of which speech is one of the external human manifestations). Such a concept of justice is valid on a cosmic level, as well as on a human level. In order to be fair, the Egyptians had to live in accordance with Maat.[263] Due to its involvement in the immaterial side of life, the Egyptian concept of justice is of great value in the context of the Internet, as the Internet also deals with the circulation of immaterial information. We can take benefit from the Egyptian concept of justice and apply it to the Internet in order to create material prosperity from the correct flow of immaterial information. The Internet, like the Egyptian justice, allows the creation of material prosperity. Through the Internet, the interest of the modern world is now more and more focused on one of the immaterial sides of life: the circulation of information, in other words communication, which is intangible by its own nature.

In fact, we shall see how the information world of the Internet -to which modern lawyers would like to apply positive laws invented for a materialistic world- reacts much better to the Egyptian concept of justice. This concept is particularly well fitted to a world of which the essential rule is: "do not obstruct the flow of information, because its circulation brings prosperity".

For this reason, the Egyptian wisdom and knowledge regarding the flow of Maat (which was also for them the flow of information through speech) can be applied to the Internet with benefit, when the Aristotelian concept of justice is irrelevant. As for the negative sides of the Internet, we can find in an Egyptian text of wisdom a means to counter them, of which we shall speak later on, while analyzing the American *Communications Decency Act*.

SUB-PART 2

EGYPTIAN JUSTICE

APPLIED TO THE INTERNET

Anna Mancini

Through the study of the ancient Egyptian concept of Maat, we have found an idea of justice which is very different from the one effective in our modern world. In today's world, justice mainly consists in sharing[264] material goods, amounts of money and honors, and in punishing people, while the aim of Egyptian justice was quite different. The Egyptian concept of justice is original and its aim is to increase life and to allow physical wealth as well as personal intangible prosperity and happiness. In the Egyptian world, the human being is part of the cosmos. As "living matter" he has the ability to receive solar energy through the heart, to transform it and to re-emit it. One of the famous way he emits solar energy is through speech: the *logos*. The ancient Egyptians had noticed that a correct flow of solar energy, transformed into words, involved growth on many levels: inner-growth, inner-happiness, outer growth through physical and material prosperity. They also noticed that the obstruction of the flow of energy involved a decrease: destruction, misery and even death. Even if archeological remains prove that Egyptians applied this knowledge to the sphere of solar energy, they did not limit themselves to that field only. The ancient Egyptians, like other ancient people, well understood the importance of the correct flow of thought. They had also understood how much physical as well as intangible exchanges bring wealth in the tangible as well as in the intangible world. This ancient people had a sound knowledge of the fact that allowing the circulation of ideas, gifts and so on, results in life flow and creates affluence. Because of the link the Egyptian justice makes between the correct circulation of speech and the creation of prosperity, this concept is naturally better fitted to the virtual world of the Internet than the traditional concept of justice is. Moreover, Egyptian justice deals with affluence, while our justice deals with a limited material world, and most often with scarcity. Our modern concept of justice is indeed unsuitable for the Internet where there is no need to share a limited number of things between people. Ideas do not need to be shared in this traditional way, as they exist in unlimited number. Giving an idea to somebody else does not impoverish the donor. Another obstacle to the application of the traditional concept of justice is the legal sovereignty of states over their respective territory linked to the difficulty of locating people in a worldwide net. However, the Egyptian concept of justice appears very useful in the context of the Internet. The information flowing through the Internet is as intangible as solar energy (transformed into speech) the Egyptians used to deal with. Both solar energy and ideas, by their intangible nature, obey the Egyptian concept of justice as well as the law of physics which we could deduce from ancient Roman law distinction between *actio in rem* and *actio in personam*. Both indeed are manifested through matter and can only be modified through matter. For example, without hardware it is impossible to act directly upon the ideas flowing through the Internet. Another example, taken from ancient Egypt, is the fact that solar energy was believed to circulate through a tangible thing: the heart. Being intangible, both ideas and solar energy need matter (a computer, a book, a drawing, the human body for the Egyptian solar energy) to be manifested. In Egypt, the more the people got, transformed and exchanged solar energy, the most prosperous they became, while in the Internet, the more information people get, transform, and exchange, the most intellectually as well as materially prosperous they become. The same principle, the link between prosperity and information flow, operates.[265] In overcoming many traditional obstacles to the flow of ideas (such as those related to time and space), the Internet gives an unprecedented boost to the circulation of information. The ancient Egyptians knew that the flow of solar energy (notably when transformed into speech) produced prosperity at all the levels of life. The increased speed of circulation of ideas through the Internet has already given place to unprecedented wealth of information. Such wealth should now involve unprecedented economic prosperity. The ancient Egyptians had understood well that the lack of solar circulation within the human group resulted in decrease, poverty, death and many kinds of disorders. Some other ancient civilizations which we believe to be primitive were also aware of the essential role played by the law of exchange which creates prosperity. Prior to verifying, through the French and American examples, the law of decrease linked to the obstruction of the information flow, we are now going to explain more fully why the law of the flow of Maat resulted in prosperity in the ancient Egyptian world. We shall also describe how other primitive tribes took benefit from the fact that speeding the exchanges increases wealth on each level of life.

CHAPTER 9

PROSPERITY AND CIRCULATION IN EGYPT AND IN "PRIMITIVE" TRIBES

The peoples of the pre-axial civilizations are generally considered to be archaic or primitive. Nevertheless they did not need the Internet to understand the essential role played by intangible exchanges. The anthropologist Marcel MAUSS has studied North and South American tribes where these intangible exchanges were embodied in the exchange of material goods. These archaic populations believed indeed that things which have belonged to someone embody and transmit a part of the "mana", of that person.[266] The tribes studied by Marcel MAUSS used to apply rituals of exchanges involving obligations to give and obligations to receive. Such rituals resulted in an increased (and compulsory) circulation of material as well as intangible things.[267] The aim of these social practices was to create not only friendship and peace, but also wealth and material prosperity.[268] A philosophy of fair behavior regarding material goods embodying a strong spiritual value, that is to say the behavior in favor of prosperity, advised not to retain these goods but to let them circulate.[269] This leads as

Marcel MAUSS asserts to a circle of exchanges.[270] Similarities with Marcel MAUSS's ideas exist in the work on Egypt by Edward BLEIBERG,[271] entitled *The Official Gift In Ancient Egypt*. Prior to studying the typical Egyptian case, this author presents the theories proposed by economic anthropologists[272] regarding preindustrial societies. One of his main conclusions is that our modern economic views, liberal or not, do not apply to the Egyptian society.[273] In Egypt there was no "economy"[274] in the modern meaning and no purely economic relationships existed. The same occurred in the tribes studied by Marcel MAUSS. There, all the aspects of life were embodied in exchanges and no purely economic exchanges could exist. Edward BLEIBERG describes how the idea of buying for resale with profit did not exist in Egypt for the remote trade.[275] Moreover there was no accumulation of the means of exchange. This author also declares that money was known very late in Egypt, where no equivalent existed for: "to buy", "to sell", and "money".[276] According to Edward BLEIBERG, the ancient Egyptian world practiced the law of exchange. Something was given in exchange for something else. The precious metals: gold, silver, copper, were used only to facilitate these exchanges. Hence, Egypt appears as a society based on exchanges, on barter, and not on buying and selling. These last concepts supposed an already existing distinction between the social and the economic spheres. In Egypt as well as in the tribes studied by Marcel MAUSS or by Bronislaw MALINOWSKI, all the aspects of life were united. There were no purely economic exchanges. The exchange was much deeper[277] and these primitive societies did not make the distinction between economy, religion and so on. All was included in the exchanges. At the heart of the ancient Egyptian exchange it is not surprising to find Maat acting as the driving force under this circulatory dynamics. Egyptologists and Historians of Religions have mainly focused their attention on the immaterial exchange of Maat. This is due to the central role it plays in the ancient Egyptian civilization. Maat is at the heart of the intangible exchanges between the Pharaoh and the sun, during the ritual of the offering of Maat. The same occurs to the sun and the creatures it feeds with Maat. During an interview, published in the scientific paper EUREKA,[278] Jean YOYOTTE has declared that "the exchange is at the heart of Egyptian civilization" and that "the whole Egyptian civilization fit into the frame of an exchange between the gods and the human beings". Nevertheless the Egyptian literature shows that the exchange of Maat is not only an exchange between gods and men. Maat is also exchanged between men and this is a main feature of the ancient Egyptian civilization. Through his concepts of "communicative solidarity" and "active solidarity", Yan ASSMANN has studied this kind of exchange in depth. Jean-Claude GOYON has also underlined the importance to the ancient Egyptians of exchange and circulation.[279] The ancient Egyptians were well aware of the bad effects of greed, which is opposite to the law of exchange. They called it "greed of the heart". The ancient Egyptians did not consider greed as a sin. To them it was a malfunctioning that could be corrected. In fact, obstructing the flow of Maat with greed or through another behavior means doing harm to oneself prior to impoverishing the wider circle of exchanges. Let us see, through the examples of the American *Communications Decency Act* and through the French experience of the Minitel, how the Egyptian concept of justice, which consists in maintaining the flow of immaterial exchanges, can be practically verified in its positive and negative effects.

CHAPTER 10

SLOWING DOWN THE INFORMATION FLOW:
THE AMERICAN EXPERIENCE

With their longing to share knowledge for free on the Internet, scholars, researchers and the first American users of the Internet[280] have unwittingly put in action a very effective lever for economy. Primitive civilizations already knew this strategic behavior through the *do ut des*[281] principle. It is thanks to this initial generous impetus which allowed a free flow of ideas over the Internet, that the Internet found its direction and a favorable ground for a rather quick worldwide expansion. The *do ut des* principle has been successfully applied by many people on the Internet. For example, the browser Netscape,[282] given for free to users, favored a multiplication of Internet users. Finally, it enriched its creator through its external economic results.[283] The same applies to browsers. When they offer free registration of web sites and free search of information, they attract a wide number of Internet users. Their frequent visits to the web sites make them very attractive for advertising.[284] This attitude allows higher and above all quicker economic effects than those which could have been obtained through charging for registration and research services. Such a success calling attitude is much more frequent on the Internet[285] than in the traditional world.[286] It has already given place to a worldwide multiplication of exchanges between people and also to economic effects which attract many other users. Unfortunately, within them not all have such a generous attitude. Some of them use the Internet for a traditional kind of business,[287] some for illegal business, some other commit varied "virtual abuses".[288] The growing Internet-involved prosperity[289] has also caught the attention of governments. They claim that their intervention has been made necessary in order to protect say consumers or minors.[290] With extreme contradiction, some governments assert their will to protect the private life of their citizens, as well as their will to control them in order to levy tax and to fight against tax avoidance.[291] While doing so, they act in opposition to the dynamics of the Internet, believing they are favoring its expansion[292] and its economic effects! The Internet can stand the coexistence of all kinds of web sites and users without major drawbacks for its expansion.[293] Today, the most serious threat to the Internet expansion comes from governments and their use of laws which were made for a physical world. Inappropriate legal interventions can contribute to turning the Internet into a space of high legal insecurity and of intrusion into private life. Though legal interventions are not welcome by many Internet users,[294] governments go on attempting to regulate the Internet. Even in the United States, where the will to create a space of freedom on the Internet has been declared by the public authorities,[295] the U.S. Congress, with the aim to protect minors against indecent publications over the Internet, has enacted in 1996 the *Communications Decency Act*. This act contains vague but coercive measures in total opposition to the expansion of the Internet. Fortunately, thanks to their experience of the new freedom due to information wealth, Internet users and E-companies reacted against the enactment of the *Communications Decency Act*. They were successful in having it declared unconstitutional by the Supreme Court on June 26 1997.[296] Thanks to the Internet, all the details of the trial can be easily accessed, notably on the EPIC's web site. EPIC was one of the major actors against the *Communications Decency Act*.[297]

The *Communications Decency Act* punished with 2 years in prison and/or a fine the intentional transmission of obscene or indecent messages to a minor aged under 18 and the fact of sending or making available to a minor under 18 any kind of message describing or depicting "in terms patently offensive as measured by community standards, sexual or excretory activities or organs". People having taken appropriate effective actions in order to control the access of minors such as: "requiring credit cards, debit account, adult access code, or adult personal identification number" were provided with affirmative defenses. The main concern of opponents to the *Communications Decency Act* was to have it declared unconstitutional, in regard with the *First amendment* on *Freedom of Speech*. Nevertheless a close reading of the details of the affair shows that some other more economy-oriented considerations have strongly influenced the course of the trial. They mainly consist in having taken into account the specific effects of the free flow of information over the Internet. The hearings let appear the many aspects of the specific functioning of the Internet, notably the fact that a free flow of information results in higher prosperity and its obstruction in economic decrease.[298] Some have argued that, in addition to its inefficiency with regard to minors' protection, the enactment of the *Communications Decency Act* would have a very negative effect on the worldwide flow of American data over the Internet. Through the American experience, we are faced with the fact that it has become impossible for States to ban the flow of specific undesirable information over their own territory. The Internet specificity renders impossible any control over content at the international level, and this reacts on the national level. The opponents of the enactment of the *Communications Decency Act* emphasized that many sexual web sites are hosted abroad and hence are accessible to American minors. Despite its purpose, the *Communications Decency Act,* faced with International Law, will never be able to protect minors against this kind of site. The Supreme Court was wise enough to admit the limit of the power of the American public authorities.[299] A ban on specific information over the Internet, such as information contrary to community standards, can take place only in case of a worldwide unanimous agreement for such a ban. Even in this instance, it would be hard to make the ban effective. Due to the variation on what is moral even within the same small country, it is very unlikely that such unanimity can be reached on this kind of issue.[300] The debates on the *Communications Decency Act* clearly show that, when no worldwide ban can exist, if a country decides to ban a selected range of information this inevitably results in negative effects on its economy. The defendants argued that the vague but coercive nature of the *Communications Decency Act* would give place to a high legal insecurity. As it would lead the American operators to strict self-censorship in order to avoid punishment, it would break the dynamics of the Internet to the United States detriment. Judicial proceedings are a serious threat in this Country and the *Communications Decency Act* is so vague that even works of art or scientific works, depicting the human body, can fall under its scope. Consequently such a legal insecurity would be a source of drawbacks for the American people, while other countries with a better legal frame would not face this problem and hence would continue to benefit from the economic dynamics of the Internet. In summary we can say that:

- Any attempt to ban information which takes place at a national level results for the attempting country in a decrease in quality and quantity of the flow of its national information on the Internet. This corresponds to a loss of information prosperity as well as physical prosperity,

- This loss of information prosperity involves as Apple and Microsoft[301] argue, a loss in the Internet-related electronic market, hence a loss of physical wealth (say a decrease in employment).

- Any inappropriate, intrusive and obstructive legal frame imposed on a country put it out of the worldwide intellectual, artistic and business flow. Such an attitude directly benefits the other countries which have understood the interest of letting information freely flow and applying the Egyptian concept of justice. That is to say that they try to set up intelligent, efficient and creative means to establish the best balance for a free flow of information over the Internet. In the minors' case, parental intervention and technical means like filtering software, can contribute to establishing a balance between the imperatives of the free information flow and the legitimate will to protect minors against undesirable contents.

Cyberspace is concerned with laws different from those of real space. We must be well aware that all the debates which have occurred regarding the obscure aspects of the Internet and which were widely featured in the media have contributed to advertise these aspects directly and to prejudice the image of the Internet.[302] The ancient Egyptians were wiser than we are when dealing with the intangible: they said that the best way to fight against darkness is to bring light. In the Internet, there is a lot of light to put at the fore. In addition there are many forms of behavior to change in the real world in order to balance it and to make such a balance influence the virtual world. Here the ancient Roman wisdom applies: if we want to purify the virtual world, let us do it through the real world, since we have no direct power on virtual things. Through the American experience as well as that of other countries we can be aware of the contradiction which consists in believing that it is possible to purify behavior within the Internet when this aim is far from being reached in the real world, ever though there we are better equipped to do it.[303]

In summary we can say that, notwithstanding the clear will to regulate the Internet in order to protect minors or consumers, any legal measure has to face the specific functioning of the Internet. By its own nature the Internet is not concerned with territories and borders, which are a prerequisite for governmental legal efficiency. It is obvious that any State forbidding any kind of information on its territory will never[304] be able to prevent its citizens from access to the same information having its sources outside the national territory. The practical inefficiency of national rules is clear.[305] In addition, it involves a slow-down in the information flow to the detriment of those countries which have a restrictive legal frame. A governmental action, too intrusive or bureaucratic with regard to the Internet, inevitably results in a diversion of the information flow and of its ensuing wealth to the benefit of other more liberal countries.[306] In these last countries, citizens not hindered by increasing legal insecurity will draw more benefits from the dynamics of the Internet. The Ancient Egyptian concept of justice can be totally verified: slowing down the circulation of information within the Internet results in decreasing the opportunities of physical as well as intangible wealth. In this regard, the French Minitel is the counter-example of the dynamics which made the Internet expand successfully worldwide. Hence it is worthwhile to study the Minitel case in order to avoid repeating the same mistakes with the same consequences within the Internet.

CHAPTER 11

HINDERING THE INFORMATION FLOW: THE FRENCH USE OF THE MINITEL

1. The *do ut des* and the launching of a new information market

On the initiative of the public powers, the Minitel was launched by the early 1980s and distributed to the users[307] for free. Thanks to this strategy, this new computer terminal[308] quickly reached homes and workplaces, and the Minitel, as a necessary tool to access Teletel services, was available to a large number of users. The French public powers subsidized this new market and declared that they aimed to use the Minitel as a means of democratization of the access to information. Furthermore, they wanted to give France a technological edge that could be exported and lucrative. The dominant objective of France Télécom,[309] then a totally State-owned company, was to stimulate French telephonic consumption which had become stagnant.[310] One of the varied aims declared by the public powers, has not actually been achieved: the democratization of access to information, in other words information

123

abundance for all. This has been true since the beginnings when this aim seemed to be widely forgotten. The initial gift of the Minitel allowed the creation of a telecommunication market, while many other countries failed in the same attempt. Unfortunately the adoption of a marketing strategy in total opposition to the *do ut des* principle led to a limitation of the Minitel's use. Only a segment of the population and of the companies which could afford this costly means of access to information actually benefited from the easier access to information permitted by the Minitel. Such a marketing strategy, as we shall study in more depth below, did not allow the generation of information wealth and its ensuing external prosperity.[311] On the contrary, this strategy contributed powerfully to making the Minitel a tool which has not been able to keep up with technological changes. Its use began to stagnate by 1994 and today it has been widely overtaken by the Internet.[312]

2. The strategy of scarcity of the "kiosk" system

When the Minitel was launched in the early 1980, France Télécom benefited from several main advantages. Though the mark-ups for the services offered through the Minitel were abusively high,[313] these advantages permitted France Télécom to be successful in the creation of an information market. These advantages were the followings:

telecommunications monopoly, public subsidization, competition-free national market.[314] Thanks to such a context, France Télécom was able to impose on the users and on the service providers the "kiosk system".[315] Under the kiosk system, the payment for the access to information is time-based and the pricing differentiated according to the kind of services proposed.[316] For example, in 1995, if a user wanted to browse the Electre data base on French books, he had to pay 131,40 French Francs per hour (about 18 USD). This amount was collected directly by France Télécom, which returned part of it to the service provider after having retained a considerable portion.[317] Hence, it is very easy to understand why the OECD economists reported the "Negative consequences of the quest for profitability"[318] involved by the kiosk system. The kiosk system appears in fact to be exactly the opposite of the *do ut des* principle. The *do ut des* logic: "I give in order that you give" implies an exchange of which the result is to enrich the whole community. The kiosk system implies the opposite logic: "the less I give, The more I earn" that impoverishes the whole community in the long term and breaks the dynamics of exchanges. The OECD economists could rightly observe:

> Today, it would appear that the kiosk system, which provided the impetus for the Minitel, has become the main obstacle to its continued growth. Users are effectively charged for the time they spend on-line and

services providers are paid accordingly. Hence, for most services, what matters is the duration of calls. The more time a caller spends on a call, the greater the return. Hence there is a tendency to make calls last longer. The Minitel format thus works in a perverse way, since simple, fast and efficient services generate less revenue than complicated, slow and inefficient ones (at least in the short run, for over time demand will inevitably drop).[319]

The main effects of the perverse use of the kiosk system are the enrichment of a few people[320] and of France Télécom and the loss, for France, of an unprecedented opportunity for economic and social growth. A more appropriate use of the Minitel and of the public funds invested in this tool would have resulted in an economic and social advantage. Through the practical example of the SNCF (national railway company),[321] we are now going to study how the kiosk system was applied in practice and its effects.

The SNCF case

When no Minitel existed, French people could get free information on train travel from the SNCF, a State-owned company. Times of departures and arrivals, prices, and information on price reduction could be obtained free by phone[322] or at the ticket offices. With the launch of the Minitel by 1982, this information ceased to be free. For the first time in the history of France, people had to pay for it through the Minitel and later on also through the telephone, according to the kiosk time-based system, which was extended to telephonic services. The logic is therefore that if people refuse to pay for that, the only way to get information is to continue queuing at the ticket offices. Though Minitel and an excellent telecommunication network have been available to French people since 1982, they still continue [323] to jam the ticket offices at railway stations. An appropriate use of the Minitel could have avoided for the SNCF the expenses of maintaining a large number of ticket offices. Such an appropriate use of the Minitel could have facilitated the life of **all** the French people, and invited them to travel more. At first sight, the SNCF easily earns money by selling its commercial information through the Minitel or over the phone,[324] but such an artificially organized scarcity results in missing a greater prosperity.[325] How many sales are missed this way? How much does it cost the SNCF to maintain the many tickets offices made artificially necessary? Let us imagine that instead of this marketing strategy, the SNCF had applied the *do ut des* which makes the Internet successful. As a public service, the SNCF could have had the legitimate will to make available its commercial information to potential travelers, for free and through any means. As a first result, queues at the ticket offices would have certainly decreased. The *do ut des* principle could have made SNCF's Minitel site a mine of prosperity.[326] Far before the existence of the Internet, it could have disseminated also information on hotels, restaurants, tour operators etc... In doing so, the SNCF would have earned much more than what it gets through the sale of its information, (which is otherwise free) to people who can afford it or are in a hurry. While meeting its public service aim it could also have earned much more, and contributed to the creation of an information wealth for all. Such an attitude would have resulted, according to the *do ut des* logic, in increased physical wealth linked to increased flow of information. Moreover, the SNCF would have contributed to the technological development the Minitel instead of contributing like all the other players to its obvious and desired technical stagnation. In effect the time-based pricing encourages the information providers to be as slow as possible in delivering information to the users in order to earn more money. Hence the uselessness of technological progress for the Minitel. Unfortunately, the SNCF is not the only company involved in the perverse use of the Minitel (and now of the phone). Many French companies and public services today go on selling through the Minitel or over the phone, according to the kiosk system, information that in their very interest and in the interest of all, should circulate as freely and as rapidly as possible. We made the choice of the SNCF insofar as it is a field particularly concerned with circulation[327] and also because it is one of the most used Minitel services. For these reasons, it is a good case study for being aware of the loss of economic prosperity and of information wealth.

In conclusion, this chapter has allowed us to check that the ancient Egyptian principle of justice, which was successfully applied by the United States in answer to the request for unconstitutionality of the *Communications Decency Act*, contributed to maintain the information flow and its ensuing prosperity. This has not been the case in France where the public authorities took no action in order to meet the initial aim of the Minitel, which was democratization of access to information. In this context, France Télécom and the majority of the players have had an "unfair" attitude in the use of the Minitel. The inappropriate and perverse use of the Minitel has not allowed France to get the best results from the use of this tool in advance of its time, which would have allowed intangible and material prosperity connected to the acceleration of the information-flow over the French territory. Through the case studies of the American *Communications Decency Act* and of the French experience with the Minitel, the practical efficiency of the Egyptian idea of justice has been verified.

CONCLUSION

As we have seen, the phenomenon of the Internet has created the need for a fundamental transformation in legal thought and behavior. We need to be innovative and to understand the new rules of the game. On the Internet, what matters is the acceleration of information flow. The dynamics of a world of informational affluence are necessarily different from those of the limited material world. In cyberspace, we no longer need to share a specified amount of physical goods, and thus the concepts of territory and territorial sovereignty of states have become irrelevant. The entire information flow is intended for people's minds and not for their bodies. In cyberspace, people, with their dreams, thoughts, relationships, and intangible needs have come to the fore of the legal stage. Thinking about the Internet is much more than economic or law-oriented thinking. It confronts us directly with the absence of a modern legal philosophy of the immaterial world. Ancient civilizations have much to teach us concerning that world, provided we open our minds to their symbolic languages and to their intuitive but nevertheless practical mentality.

The main effect of the Internet seems to be its action on the collective psyche. It destroys age-old bearings and obliges us to behave differently and to consider life with new eyes. The Internet is only a tool, but a wonderful tool. We must hope it will be used for the best.

NOTES

1. Any kind of censorship, in other words the Internet frees the manifestation of the human thought from all the traditional obstacles permitted by matter and through matter by the traditional institutions.

2. LESSIG Lawrence, *Code And Other Laws Of Cyberspace*, NY, Basic Books, 1999, p. 108.

3. LESSIG Lawrence, *op. cit.*, p. 185.

4. LESSIG Lawrence, *op. cit.*, p. 111: "...translation alone will not be enough; the past will not resolve the future. The questions raised by the future are issues that were not decided in the past."

5. VILLEY Michel, *Le Droit Romain*, PUF, Que sais-je?, 1979, p. 119.

6. By "traditional world" we mean the world without the Internet.

7. ROUSSEAU Jean-Jacques, *Discourse On The Origin Of Inequality,* translated by Franklin PHILIP, Oxford, NY, Oxford University Press, 1994, p. 55.

8. This link is also underlined by Pierre GRIMAL regarding ancient Rome, GRIMAL Pierre, *La civilisation romaine*, Paris, Champs, Flammarion, 1997, p. 193.

9. PELT Jean-Marie, *La vie sociale des plantes*, Paris, Fayard, 1984, p. 91, p. 138, p. 149, p. 150, p. 153, p. 156; p. 157, p. 160, p. 164, p. 175, pp. 262-263.

10 Regarding animals *cf.* Jean-Marie PELT, *op. cit.,* p. 150 and p. 222.

11. MOLYNEAUX Brian Leigh, *The Sacred Earth*, London, Macmillan, 1995, p. 44 and following pages.

12. We translate it from the French text quoted by Ghislain OTIS and Bjarne MELKEVICK: "L'universalisme moderne à l'heure des identités: le défi singulier des peuples autochtones", in *Les Droits Fondamentaux*, BRUYLANT BRUXELLES, 1997, ACTES des 1ères Journées scientifiques du Réseau Droits fondamentaux de l'AUPELF-UREF: p. 274 and following pages.
Charte de la Terre des peuples autochtones du Canada:

Art 31: "Les peuples autochtones ont été placés sur notre mère, la Terre, par le Créateur. Nous appartenons à la terre. Nous ne pouvons être séparés de nos terres et de nos territoires".

"Nos territoires sont des entités vivantes qui s'inscrivent dans une relation vitale permanente entre les êtres humains et la nature."

[13] ARDEN Harvey, *Noble Red Man, Mathew King, un sage Lakota*, translation from American by Karin BODSON, Paris, Editions du Rocher, 1994, p. 101, quotation translated from the French text: "Seul Dieu est notre Père, et la Terre est notre Mère. Nous en avons la preuve car notre peau est de la couleur de Terre-Mère".

[14]. MAGNANT Jean-Pierre, *Terre et pouvoir dans les populations dites "Sara" du Sud du Tchad*, Paris I, thesis political sciences, 1983.

[15]. MAGNANT Jean-Pierre, *op. cit.*, p. 148

[16]. MAGNANT Jean-Pierre, *op. cit.*, p. 159 and pp. 160-161.

[17]. MAGNANT Jean-Pierre, *op. cit.*, p. 150.

[18]. MAGNANT Jean-Pierre, *op. cit.*, p. 156.

[19]. MAGNANT Jean-Pierre, *op. cit.*, p. 156.

[20]. MAGNANT Jean-Pierre, *op. cit.*, p. 197.

[21]. MAGNANT Jean-Pierre, *op. cit.*, p. 169.

[22]. MAGNANT Jean-Pierre, *op. cit.*, pp. 171-172.

[23]. MAGNANT Jean-Pierre, *op. cit.*, pp. 156-157.

[24] MAGNANT Jean-Pierre, *op. cit.*, p. 170.

[25]. KELSEN Hans, *Théorie Pure du Droit, Introduction à la Science du Droit*, Neuchâtel, Editions de la Baconnière, 1953, translated from German by Henri Thévenaz, German title *Reine Rechtslehre*, 1934. When not indicated the footnotes refer to the French version of the *Pure Theory of Law*. In the French version Hans KELSEN made some changes not appearing in the English translation we used. Some quotations are from the following English translation of the *Pure Theory of Law*: KELSEN Hans, *Introduction To The Problems Of Legal Theory, A translation of the First Edition of the Reine Rechtslehre or Pure Theory Of Law*, translated by Bonnie LITSCHEVESKI PAULSON and Stanley L. PAULSON, Oxford, Clarendon Press, 1992.

[26]. KELSEN Hans, *Introduction To The Problems Of Legal Theory, A translation of the First Edition of the Reine Rechtslehre or Pure Theory Of Law*, translated by Bonnie LITSCHEVESKI PAULSON and Stanley L. PAULSON, Oxford, Clarendon Press, 1992, p. 2 and p. 26.

[27]. KELSEN Hans, *op. cit.*, p. 7.

[28]. KELSEN Hans, *op. cit.*, p. 17 and p. 56.

[29]. KELSEN Hans, *op. cit.*, pp. 12-14 and p. 17.

30. KELSEN Hans, *op. cit.*, p. 59.

31. KELSEN Hans, *op. cit.*, pp. 53-54-55.

32. KELSEN Hans, *op. cit.*, p. 111.

33. KELSEN Hans, *op. cit.*, p. 64.

34. KELSEN Hans, *op. cit.*, p. 142.

35. KELSEN Hans, *op. cit.*, p. 13.

36. KELSEN Hans, *op. cit.*, p. 43.

37. KELSEN Hans, *op. cit.*, pp. 50-51, and p. 53.

38. KELSEN Hans, *op. cit.*, pp. 43-44.

39. But the concept of imputation is not scientific, it is an act of will.

40. KELSEN Hans, *op. cit.*, p. 53.

41. KELSEN Hans, *op. cit.*, p. 19, *cf.* also: pp. 88-89 and pp. 88-89.

42. KELSEN Hans, English translation, *op. cit.*, p. 12.

43. KELSEN Hans, English translation, *op. cit.*, p. 12.

44. KELSEN Hans, *op. cit*, p. 42.

45. KELSEN Hans, *op. cit.*, p. 166 and following pages. On the State as a point of imputation see pp. 157-158.

46. KELSEN Hans, *op. cit.*, p. 154.

47. KELSEN Hans, *op. cit.*, p. 120. See also his last chapter on the International Law.

48. KELSEN Hans, *op. cit.*, p. 173.

49. KELSEN Hans, English translation, *op. cit.*, p. 124.

50. KELSEN Hans, *op. cit.*, p. 168 and p. 184.

51. KELSEN Hans, *op. cit.*, p. 173 and p. 183.

52. KELSEN Hans, *op. cit.*, p. 176.

53. KELSEN Hans, English translation, *op. cit.*, pp. 120-121.

54. For a view of the new trends in philosophy of law *cf.* Bjarne MELKEVIK, *Horizons de la philosophie du droit*, L'Harmattan, PUL, Paris, Montréal, 1998.

55. *Cf* the articles of FLORY Maurice, MERLE Marcel etc... quoted below in *L'international sans territoire*, *op. cit.*, Paris, L'Harmattan, 1996; *cf.* VERHOEVEN Joe, "Souveraineté et mondialisation: libres propos", in *La mondialisation du droit*, Edited by Eric LOQUIN and Catherine KESSEDJIAN, Travaux du Centre de Recherche sur le droit des

marchés et des investissements internationaux, Book 19, LITEC, 2000, pp. 43-57, p. 49 and 57.

[56]. MERLE Marcel, "Un système international sans territoire?", *L'international sans territoire, op. cit.*, L'Harmattan, 1996, p. 289 and p. 290.

[57]. FLORY Maurice, "Le couple Etat-territoire en droit international contemporain", in *L'international sans territoire, op. cit.,* p. 251 and following pages.

[58]. *Ibid*, p. 252.

[59]. FLORY Maurice, "Le couple Etat-territoire en droit international contemporain", *op. cit.*, p. 264.

[60]. Marcel MERLE, "Un système international sans territoire?", *L'international sans territoire, op. cit.,* p. 289 and following pages, p. 291.

[61]. *Cf.* Marcel MERLE, *op. cit.*, p. 295.

[62]. Dans ce sens: VERHOEVEN Joe, "Souveraineté et mondialisation: libres propos", in *La mondialisation du droit, op. cit.*, pp. 43-57, p. 46, p. 49. Regarding the consequences of the crisis of territoriality on the authors' right *cf.* GELLER Paul Edward, "Conflicts Of Law In Cyberspace: International Copyright In A Digitally Networked World", in *The Future Of Copyright In A Digital Environment*, editor P. Bernt HUGENHOLTZ, Proceedings of the Royal Academy Colloquium, Amsterdam, 6-7 July 1995, KLUWER LAW INTERNATIONAL, The hague, London, Boston, 1996, pp. 27-48, p. 48.

[63]. ANDREFF Wladimir, "La déterritorialisation des multi-nationales: firmes globales et firmes réseaux", in *L'international sans territoire, op. cit.*, L'Harmattan, 1996, p. 373 and following pages.

[64]. ANDREFF Wladimir, *op. cit.,* p. 392.

[65]. CARNOI Martin, CASTELLS Manuel, COHEN Stephen S., CARDOSO Fernando Henrique, *The New Global Economy In The Information Age*, the Pensylvania State University Press, The MACMILLAN PRESS LTD, 1993.

[66]. BALLE Francis, *Médias et Sociétés, de Gutenberg à Internet*, Paris, Montchrestien.

[67]. BALLE Francis, *op. cit.*, p. 699.

[68]. On the economic definition on the word globalization *cf.* VERHOEVEN Joe, "Souveraineté et mondialisation: libres propos", in *La mondialisation du droit, op. cit.*, pp. 43-57, p. 45.

[69]. For example, regarding the legal obligation to use the French language for French people, the Conseil d'Etat, in its report reckons the impossibility to apply such a law in some Internet contexts, especially

when advertising reaching the French consumers was not specifically intended for them. Conseil d'Etat, France, *Internet et les réseaux numériques, étude adoptée par l'Assemblée générale du Conseil d'Etat, 2 July 1998*, Paris, La Documentation française, 1998, p. 35 and following pages.

[70]. KRUSE Frederik Vinding, *The Right Of Property*, London, New York, Toronto, Oxford University Press, 1939, p. 80. For a recent analysis in the same line *cf.* James Dale DAVIDSON and William REES-MOGG, *The Sovereign Individual, The Coming Economic Revolution*, London, MACMILLAN, 1997.

[71]. KRUSE Frederik Vinding, *op. cit.*, p. 80.

[72]. KRUSE Frederik Vinding, *op. cit.*, p. 75, he speaks about the intellectual rights and explains it as follows: "The sphere which should presumably correctly be attributed to the intellectual property rights covers authors' and artists' copyrights, patent rights, and the rights of designs, but this is not claimed to be an exhaustive enumeration; new kinds of non-material property are continually developing and the types hitherto acknowledged are constantly being extended to cover more and more ground".

[73]. KRUSE Frederik Vinding, *op. cit.*, p. 75.

[74]. KRUSE Frederik Vinding, *op. cit.*, pp. 107-109.

[75]. We do not give here the definition of a material right (droit réel) or of a personal right (droit personnel). These concepts have given place to vivid scholarly disputes of which we shall speak more in depth in the chapter dedicated to the theories of the distinction between material and personal rights. For now we just need to say that we are dealing with material subjective rights and personal subjective rights as they exist in the actual continental positive laws.

[76]. VILLEY Michel, *Le Droit Romain, op. cit.*, p. 19.

[77]. We can find the French Civil Code as well as French legal information on the web site: http://www.legifrance.gouv.fr.

[78]. In this line, *cf.* François TERRÉ, *Introduction Générale au Droit*, Dalloz, Paris, 1998, p. 61.

[79]. In this line, *cf.* François TERRÉ, *Introduction Générale au Droit*, Dalloz, Paris, 1998, p. 62.

[80]. *Cf.* the definitions given in the *Lexique des termes juridiques*, Dalloz, 1988, p. 56, p. 83, p. 241, pp. 298-299.

[81]. VILLEY Michel, *Le Droit Romain, op. cit.*, p. 76.

[82]. VILLEY Michel, *Le Droit Romain, op. cit.*, p. 70.

[83]. VILLEY Michel, "Les origines de la notion de droit subjectif", *Archives de Philosophie du Droit*, Paris, Recueil SIREY, 1953-54, pp.

163-187, p. 167. On the distortion of Roman Law *cf.*: VILLEY Michel, "La notion romaine classique de *Jus* et le *Dikaion* d'Aristote", *La filosofia greca e il diritto romano*, Roma, Accademia Nazionale dei Lincei, 1976, pp. 71-79, p. 76.

[84]. On the Middle Ages origin of this say and its introduction in the French Civil Code in 1804, *cf.*: ROLAND Henri, BOYER Laurent, *Adages du droit français*, Paris, Litec, 1999, p. 796; TERRÉ François, *Introduction Générale au Droit*, Paris Dalloz, 1998, pp. 342-343-344.

[85]. VILLEY Michel, *Le Droit Romain*, *op. cit.*, p. 76.

[86]. On the basis of which the Ancient Romans built the distinction between *actio in rem* and *actio in personam*.

[87]. Software was the object of vivid discussion about the right protection they could be afforded and about their legal definition. Finally they have paradoxically been assimilated to literature and are protected, of course imperfectly, under copyright laws.

[88]. WHINSTON Andrew B., STAHL Dale O., CHOI Soon-Yong, *The Economics of Electronic Commerce,* Indianapolis, Indiana, Macmillan Technical Publishing, 1997, pp. 178-179: "Despite being called "property," intellectual properties are obviously quite different from tangible properties, and therefore legal protection and prosecution based on copyright law are substantially different from other property laws."

[89]. The French Code of Intellectual property (Code de la propriété intellectuelle) states (article L. 111-1) in its chapter dedicated to the nature of the author's right: "The author of a work of the mind enjoys on this work, as soon as it is created, a right of incorporeal property exclusive and opposable to all" and explains (in Article L. 111-3) "The incorporeal property defined in the Article L. 111-1 is independent from the property of the tangible thing".(translated from French texts: "L'auteur d'une oeuvre de l'esprit jouit sur cette oeuvre, du seul fait de sa création, d'un droit de propriété incorporelle exclusif et opposable à tous". et précise (à l'article L. 111-3): "La propriété incorporelle définie par l'article L. 111-1 est indépendante de la propriété de l'objet matériel").

[90]. Pierre BOURDIEU could compare law to a successful magical action, BOURDIEU Pierre *Ce que parler veut dire, l'économie des échanges linguistiques*, Paris, Fayard, 1982, p. 20.

[91]. *Cf.* WIPO Copyright Treaty, Geneva, December 1996, article 6 On the Right of distribution (French text). No analysis of the nature of the author's right is attempted in the preamble.

[92]. Later on, we shall study more in depth the Roman distinction between *actio in rem* and *actio in personam*.

[93]. According to Michel VILLEY, natural obligations exist prior to the legal ones: "Métamorphoses de l'obligation", *Archives de Philosophie du*

droit, Communication au congrès de l'Institut International de Philosophie politique sur "l'obligation politique", 4 July 1969, p. 297.

[94]. See the example of Vivendi and Suez Lyonnaise in les Echos, 13 July 2000, Paris, p. 1 and pp. 12-13.

[95]. Even if some contents are at a low level and should be improved.

[96]. Regarding the evolution of the electronic commerce *cf*: GUÉRIN Serge, *Internet en questions*, Paris, Economica, 1997, p. 87, p. 91, p. 71, p. 86.

[97]. ANDREFF Wladimir, "La déterritorialisation des multi-nationales: firmes globales et firmes réseaux", *op. cit.*, 1996, p. 392.

[98]. This phenomenon is broadly echoed in the newspapers headlines, for example see: France Soir about David Filo and Jerry Yang, inventors of Yahoo: France Soir, Paris, 22 December 1999, pp. 1-3. On the forecasts on electronic commerce in 2003 *cf*. IDC and Center for Research in electronic Commerce - University of Texas, quoted in *Les cahiers de l'économie digitale*, December 1999, p. 8. On the success of Netscape, *cf.*: QUITTNER Joshua and SLATALLA Michelle, *Speeding The Net*, London, Orion Business Books, 1998.

[99]. For a definition of the word *persona cf.*: BREAL Michel and BAILLY Anatole, *Dictionnaire étymologique latin*, Paris, Hachette, 1898, p. 260.

[100]. MAUSS Marcel, *Sociologie et anthropologie*, Paris, PUF/QUADRIGE, 1999 "Essai sur le don" pp. 143-279., Extrait de l'Année Sociologique, 1923-1924, Book I., p. 350.

[101]. TRIGEAUD Jean-Marc, *Persona ou la justice au double visage*, Genova, Studio Editoriale di Cultura, 1997, p. 49.

[102]. TZITZIS Stamatios, *Qu'est-ce que la personne?*, Paris, Armand Colin, 1999, p. 9, p. 10.

[103]. We shall study later more in depth the Roman distinction between *actio in rem* and *actio in personam*.

[104]. LEVI-STRAUSS Claude, *La voie des masques*, Paris, Editions PLON, collection Agora, 1979, p. 21 on masks as purification means, p. 24 on masks as healing means.

[105]. LEVI-STRAUSS Claude, *op. cit.*, p. 57.

[106]. On the word magic, *cf.* JUNG C.G., *Dialectique du Moi et de l'inconscient*, Paris, Gallimard, collection Folio, Essai 1964, translated from German by Doctor Roland CAHEN, p. 137.

[107]. SARRAF Joseph, *La notion du droit d'après les Anciens Egyptiens*, Rome, Città del Vaticano, Libreria editrice vaticana,1984, Collana storia e attualità, no 10, p. 41.

[108]. SARRAF Joseph, *op. cit.*, p. 41.

[109]. TZITZIS Stamatios, *Esthétique de la Violence*, Paris, PUF, 1997, p. 81, translated from French: "Le corps se révèle dès lors comme le fondement de la personne; c'est par le corps que se manifeste la personnalité. Quand bien même on ne le mentionne et qu'il paraît être absent, le corps marque implicitement sa présence. Ceci est évident dans les dispositions du Code pénal. Le deuxième livre est consacré aux crimes et aux délits contre les personnes. Notamment, son deuxième titre se rapporte aux 'atteintes à la personne humaine'. Certes, la personne humaine comporte, pour le droit, une dimension physique, et une autre, psychique. Mais le principe de la vie, avant d'exprimer un état d' *animus* passe par le corps. Ainsi lorsque le législateur définit le crime, il vise d'abord le corps. L'attentat à la vie humaine concerne plus l'agression du corps et beaucoup moins celle de l'âme. Pour le droit qui ignore la pensée désincarnée, c'est le corps que l'on peut supprimer et non l'âme.

[110]. According to the philosopher Karl JASPERS, the "axial period" can be dated around 500 B.C. It is this "axial period" which forms the basis of our universal history. We ever return to this basis from which we draw our values and inspirations. During this period Men began rejecting myths and magic and developed their rational minds *Cf.* Karl JASPERS, *Origine et sens de l'histoire*, translated from the German by Hélène NAEF and Wolfgang ACHTERBERG, Plon, Paris, 1954 (German title: *Von Urprung un Ziel der Geschitchte*), *cf.* especially for the definition and the main features of the "axial period": pp. **8-10**, 18, 31, 68, 80, 93, 174, **330**.

[111]. On the opinion that there is no legal gap and that the positive laws should apply to the Internet, *cf.* Valérie SéDALLIAN, *Droit de l'Internet*, Paris, Net Press, collection AUI, 1997, On the cover of this book, in the same line: Alain WEBER; Olivier ITEANU, *Internet et le droit, Aspect juridiques du commerce électronique*, Paris, Eyrolles, 1996, p. 8; Pierre BRESSE, Gautier KAUFMAN, *Guide juridique de l'internet et du commerce électronique*, Paris, Vuibert, 2000, p. 15; *Internet, Aspects juridiques*, editor Alain BENSOUSSAN, Paris, Hermès, 1996, p. 11; Jean MARTIN, "Le cyberespace: un prétendu vide juridique", Le Monde, 3 May 1996, p. 15. The quote would be endless as it is logical that positivistic lawyers do not like legal gaps. *Cf.* on lawyers refusing legal gaps: Jean-Pierre CLAVIER, *Les catégories de la propriété intellectuelle à l'épreuve des créations génétiques*, Paris and Montréal, L'Harmattan, 1998, p. 18, Hans KELSEN, *op. cit.,* p. 147.

[112]. Despite the progress permitted by CHAMPOLLION in the field of Egyptology, Roman Law scholars still only use the information stemming from the axial Greco-Roman period and do not take into account the new light on remote civilizations that Egyptology has brought. The knowledge gained through the progress of Egyptology makes today obvious the link between the archaic Roman thought and the Egyptian thought. If Greece allows a better understanding of classical Roman Law, Egypt permits a better understanding of primitive Roman Law. Despite the poor interest manifested by Roman Law scholars with

regard to Egyptology we can find some of them who remained isolated in their interest in linking the ancient Egypt to the ancient Roman law, *cf.* Eugène REVILLOUT, *Les origines égyptiennes du droit civil romain*, Paris, Librairie Paul Geuthner, 1912; Paul HUVELIN, *Les tablettes magiques et le droit romain*, Macon, Protat Frères, 1901, p. 5.

[113]. In the continental legal systems.

[114]. And on the ancient Roman legal impact on the virtual side of life.

[115]. As the distinction between material and personal rights is fundamental it has given place to a very abundant doctrine. Therefore the references we give below are not exhaustive as this question is still debated today especially in relation with intellectual property.

[116]. **For a detailed study of the different theories proposed until the end of the nineteenth century**, *cf.* MICHAS H. *Le droit réel considéré comme une obligation passivement universelle*, Paris, thesis,1900, This authors gives a detailed bibliography as follows: Charles TOULLIER, *Le droit civil français*, Paris, 5e éd., 1830, Book III, p. 55, n° 84; Alexandre DURANTON, *Cours de droit français*, Paris, 1828, book IV, p. 182, n° 225; MARCADé, *Explication du Code Civil*, Paris, 1886, book II, p. 364, n° 357; DEMOLOMBE, *Cours de Code Napoléon*, Paris, 1854, book IX, p. 354; AUBRY ET RAU *Cours de droit civil français*, Paris, book II, 1897, p. 72 and p. 73, n° 172; BOITEUX, *Commentaire sur le Code Napoléon*, Paris, 1852, Book II, pp. 645-647; DELVINCOURT, *Cours de droit civil*, Paris, 1825, Book II, p. 309; BAUDRY-LACANTINERIE, *Précis de droit civil*, Paris, Book I, p. 646 and following pages; BOISTEL, *Cours de philosophie du droit*, Paris, 2 books, 1899; LESENNE, *De la propriété avec ses démembrements*, Paris, 1858, p. 200, n° 396; MOURLON ET DEMANGEAT, *Répétitions écrites sur le Code Civil*, Paris, 1896, book I, p. 718. **On the doctrine of the beginning of the twentieth century**, *cf.* RIGAUD Louis, *Le droit réel, histoire et théories, son origine institutionnelle*, Toulouse, thesis, 1912; RIPERT Georges, *De l'exercice du droit de propriété dans ses rapports avec les propriétés voisines*, Aix, thesis, 1902; QUERU R., *Synthèse du droit réel et du droit personnel - Essai d'une critique historique et théorique du réalisme juridique*, Caen, thesis, 1905; PRODAN C., *Essai d'une théorie générale des droits réels*, Paris, thesis, 1909; DEMOGUE René, *Les notions fondamentales du*

droit privé, Essai critique pour servir d'introduction à l'étude des obligations, Paris, Rousseau, 4 books, 1911; PLANIOL Marcel *Traité élémentaire de droit civil*, Paris, Pichon, 3 Books, 1908; CAPITANT Henri, *Introduction à l'étude du droit civil*, Paris, 1904, pp. 77-78; DABIN Jean "Les droits intellectuels comme catégorie juridique", Revue critique de législation et de jurisprudence, 1939. On the study of this distinction in regard with the authors rights and intellectual property *cf.* RECHT Pierre, *Le droit d'auteur, une nouvelle forme de propriété*, Paris, LGDJ, 1969, passim; KRUSE Frederik Vinding, *The right of property*, London, New York, Toronto, Oxford University Press, 1939.

117. **For more recent opinions,** *cf.* DERUPPÉ Jean, *La nature juridique du droit du preneur à bail et la distinction des droits réels et des droits de créance*, Paris, Dalloz, 1952; ABERKANE Hassen, *Contribution à l'étude de la distinction des droits de créance et des droits réels*, Paris, LGDJ, 1957; MARTY (G) et RAYNAUD (P), *Droit civil, Introduction générale à l'étude du droit*, Paris, SIREY, 1972, p. 482, n° 302, GINOSSAR Samuel, *Droit réel, propriété et créance - élaboration d'un système rationnel des droits patrimoniaux*, Paris, LGDJ, 1960; BOQUET Claude, *De l'opposabilité aux tiers comme caractéristique du droit réel: essai d'épistémologie juridique sur la base des droits allemand, français et suisse*, Genève, Avenir, 1978; LEVIS Marc, *l'Opposablité du droit réel*, thesis, Paris II, 1985.

118. As an example we quote the following basic books: TERRÉ François, *Introduction Générale au Droit*, Paris, Dalloz, 1998, p. 347; TERRÉ François, SIMLER Philippe, LEQUETTE Yves, *Droit civil, les obligations*, Paris, Dalloz, 1999, n° 3; VOIRIN Pierre, *Droit civil*, Book 1, Paris, L.G.D.J., 1999, p. 30. Regarding German Law *cf.* EBKE Werner F., FINKIN Matthew W., *Introduction to German Law*, The Hague, London, Boston, Kluwer Law International, 1996, p. 229: "As explained in the legislative history of the Civil Code, it is characteristic of rights *in rem*, the subject matter of *Sachenrecht*, to be 'absolute'. This means that these rights are effective with respect to anyone who interferes with the thing in fact, i.e. by depriving the titleholder of his possession or trespassing against his possession, or in law by means of legal transactions regarding the thing. This is the main difference between rights *in rem* and obligatory rights. The latter bind only the parties privy to the contractual relation; they do not, in principle, offer the creditor a defense to a claim by a third party to whom the property -the object of the obligation- has been transferred. In contrast, a right *in rem* is 'absolute' and assertable with respect to the material object even though it had been the subject of such a transfer."

[119]. He is a Danish professor of law: KRUSE Frederik Vinding, *The Right of Property*, London, New York, Toronto, Oxford University Press, 1939, p. 124.

[120]. *Ibid.*, p. 125: "Hence we might also avoid in future all those speculative inquiries which now encumber legal works on the principles of the law of 'material rights' or 'obligatory' rights".

[121]. *Ibid.*, p. 125: "Hence we might also avoid in future all those speculative inquiries which now encumber legal works on the principles of the law of 'material rights' or 'obligatory' rights".

[122]. Hans KELSEN, *op. cit*, p. 100.

[123]. As we could not get René DEMOGUE's book we are working with the quote we found in RIGAUD's work: RIGAUD Louis Hortensius, *Le droit réel, histoire et théories, son origine institutionnelle*, Toulouse, thesis, 1912, p. 179.

[124]. Louis Hortensius RIGAUD, *op. cit*, p. 196.

[125]. Even if we can still find some legal thesis on this topic.

[126]. For example, *cf.* VOIRIN Pierre, *Droit civil*, Paris, L.G.D.J, Book 1, 1999, p. 30 and following pages.

[127]. PLANIOL Marcel, *Traité élémentaire de droit civil*, Paris, Pichon, Book 1, 1908-1910, n° 2162.

[128]. The general concept of subjective right was according to Michel VILLEY an invention made during the sixteenth and seventeenth centuries *Cf.* VILLEY Michel, "Les origines de la notion de droit subjectif", Archives de Philosophie du Droit, Paris, Recueil SIREY, 1953-54, p. 163-187, p. 167; VILLEY Michel, *Suum jus cuique tribuens*, Milano, Giuffré, 1954, p. 362.

[129]. In this line: KRUSE Frederik Vinding, *The Right Of Property*, *op. cit.*, p. 130. Unfortunately the author does not pay enough attention to the Roman distinction and focuses his researches on the classical Roman Law.

[130]. According to Michel VILLEY, from the sixteenth and seventeenth centuries onward Roman Law scholars have tacked upon Roman law their own philosophy. Which led to distort Roman Law, VILLEY Michel, *Suum jus cuique tribuens*, Milano, Giuffré, 1954, passim. *Cf* on the distortion of classical Roman law: VILLEY Michel, *Suum jus cuique tribuens*, Milano, Giuffré, 1954, p. 366, 368 and 370; Michel VILLEY, "La notion romaine classique de *Jus* et le *Dikaion* d'Aristote", La filosofia greca e il diritto romano, Roma, Accademia Nazionale dei Lincei, 1976, p. 71-79, p. 71, p. 76; VILLEY Michel, "Métamorphoses de l'obligation", *Archives de Philosophie du droit*, Communication au congrès de l'Institut International de Philosophie politique sur "l'obligation politique", 4 July 1969, p. 288.

[131]. PAZZOLINI L., *La nuova scuola*, 1965, p. 423, quoted by Michel VILLEY, in "Métamorphoses de l'obligation", *Archives de Philosophie du droit*, Communication au congrès de l'Institut International de Philosophie politique sur "l'obligation politique", 4 July 1969.

[132]. POTHIER, *OEUVRES*, Paris, 1847, t. IX

[133]. MICHAS H., *Le droit réel considéré comme une obligation passivement universelle*, thesis, Paris 1900, p. 59, the author has effected an exhaustive study of the French doctrine and has quoted many tenants of this doctrine, especially: TOULLIER Charles, *Le droit civil français*, Paris, 1830, Book III, p. 55, n° 84; DURANTON, *Cours de droit français*, Paris, 1828, Book IV, p. 182, n° 225; MARCADé, *Explication du Code Civil*, Paris, 1886, Book II, p. 364, n° 357; DEMOLOMBE, *Cours de Code Napoléon*, Paris, 1854, Book IX, p. 354; AUBRY ET RAU, *Cours de droit civil français*, Book II, Paris, 1897, p. 72 and p. 73, n° 172; BOITEUX, *Commentaire sur le Code Napoléon*, Paris, 1852, Book II, pp. 645-647; DELVINCOURT, *Cours de droit civil*, Paris 1825, Book II, p. 309; BAUDRY-LACANTINERIE, *Précis de droit civil*, Book I, p. 646 and following; BOISTEL, *Cours de philosophie du droit*, 2 Books, Paris, 1899; LESENNE, *De la propriété avec ses démembrements*, Paris, 1858, p. 200, n° 396; MOURLON ET DEMANGEAT, *Répétitions écrites sur le Code Civil*, Paris, 1896, Book I, p. 718. For more recent studies *cf.*: CAPITANT Henri, *Introduction à l'étude du droit civil*, 2e éd., 1904, pp. 77-78; DABIN Jean "Les droits intellectuels comme catégorie juridique", Revue critique de législation et de jurisprudence, 1939; MARTY G. et RAYNAUD P., *Droit civil, Introduction générale à l'étude du droit*, SIREY, 1972, p. 482, n° 302.

[134]. PLANIOL Marcel, *Traité élémentaire de droit civil*, Paris, Pichon, 3 Books, 1908.

[135]. For some examples, *cf.* note n° 122.

[136]. Quotation from RIGAUD Louis, *op. cit*, p. 196.

[137]. *Cf.* KRUSE Frederik Vinding, *The Right Of Property*, *op. cit.*, 1939; GINOSSAR Samuel, *Droit réel, propriété et créance - élaboration d'un système rationnel des droits patrimoniaux*, Paris, LGDJ, 1960, p. 45.

[138]. GINOSSAR Samuel, *op. cit.*, p. 112.

[139]. PICARD Edmond, *Le droit pur - Cours d'Encyclopédie du droit- les permanences juridiques abstraites*, Paris, éd. Félix Alcan, 1899.

[140]. *Ibid*, p. 109.

[141]. PICARD Edmond, *Le droit pur - Cours d'Encyclopédie du droit- les permanences juridiques abstraites*, Paris, éd. Félix Alcan, 1899. Words translated from French.

[142]. KRUSE Frederik Vinding, *op. cit.*, pp. 107-110.

[143]. KRUSE Frederik Vinding, *op. cit.,* p. 107 "... the right of property is normally a definite set of powers."

[144]. KRUSE Frederik Vinding, *op. cit.,* p. 109 "...the powers are broadly speaking constant, the object of the powers, the goods on which the powers react, vary considerably and over a wide field. Powers... do not vary because the object instead of being an external object such as real or movable property may be an invention, a design, a trade-mark."

[145]. Louis JOSSERAND was one of the leaders of the theory of the incorporeal property *cf.* JOSSERAND Louis, "Configuration du droit de propriété dans l'ordre juridique nouveau", Mélanges juridiques, dédiés à Monsieur le Professeur SUGIYAMA, TOKIO, 1940.

[146]. *Cf.* DABIN Jean, "Les droits intellectuels comme catégorie juridique", Paris, Revue critique de législation et de jurisprudence, 1939.

[147]. KOHLER, in BONNET (J), *Etude de la législation allemande sur les brevets d'invention*, Paris, Thesis, 1902.

[148]. ROUBIER Paul, *Droit de la propriété industrielle*, Paris, Sirey, book I, p. 102; ROUBIER Paul, *Droits subjectifs et situations juridiques,* Paris, Dalloz, 1963.

[149]. VILLEY Michel, "Historique de la nature des choses", Paris, Archives de Philosophie du droit, book X, 1965, p. 267-283, p. 277.

[150]. VILLEY Michel, "Métamorphoses de l'obligation", Paris, Archives de Philosophie du droit, Communication au congrès de l'Institut International de Philosophie politique sur "l'obligation politique", 4 July 1969, p. 291.

[151]. KIERKEGAARD Sören, *The Concept Of Dread,* translated by Walter LOWRIE, Princeton, Princeton university Press, 1967, p. 39. *Cf* also p. 76 and p. 79.

[152]. KANT Immanual, *The Science Of Right*, translated by W. HASTIE, http://www.eserver.org.

[153]. On the practical dimension of the ancient Roman Law and on the fact that law, morals and religion were a whole, *cf.* CATALANO Pierangelo, *Diritto e Personne, Studi su origine e attualità del sistema romano*,Torino, G. GIPAIICHELLI EDITORE, 1990, pp. VIII-IX and p. XIII.

[154]. MICHAS H, *op. cit.*, p. 61; *cf.* also VILLEY Michel, *Le Droit Romain, op. cit.,* p. 44.

[155]. On the ancient Roman legal vocabulary and its link with magic, HUVELIN Paul, *Les tablettes magiques et le droit romain*, Macon, Protat Frères, 1901, p. 32 and p. 32 note 3. Compare with VILLEY Michel, "Métamorphoses de l'obligation", *op. cit.*, p. 269 on the English word "law". On natural obligations *cf.* Michel VILLEY, "Métamorphoses de l'obligation", *op. cit*, p. 297.

[156]. Anyone can access the registrars of patents at the Patent office, which allows "stealing" the invention. The same kind of remark has been made by some economists regarding authors' rights: WHINSTON Andrew B., STAHL Dale O., CHOI Soon-Yong, *The Economics of Electronic Commerce, op. cit.*, p. 179.

[157]. GRIMAL Pierre, *La civilisation romaine*, Paris, Champs, Flammarion, 1997.

[158]. MICHAS H., *op. cit.*, p. 31.

[159]. MICHAS H., *ibid*, p. 41, quoting: VAN BEMMELEN, *Les notions fondamentales du droit civil*, Amsterdam, 1892, p. 222.

[160]. GINOSSAR Samuel, *Droit réel, propriété et créance - élaboration d'un système rationnel des droits patrimoniaux*, Paris, LGDJ, 1960, p. 45.

[161]. VILLEY Michel, "Historique de la nature des choses", Arch. 1965, p. 276.

[162]. VILLEY Michel, *ibid.*, p. 276, p. 278.

[163]. VILLEY Michel, "Le raisonnement juridique dans l'histoire", ARSP, Arch. 1971, p. 47.

[164]. As we want to do it today when we speak about incorporeal property.

[165]. VILLEY Michel, "Historique de la nature des choses", Arch. 1965, X, p. 272.

[166]. *Ibid.*

[167]. I.e. full power on a thing; *cf.* VILLEY Michel, *Le droit romain, op. cit.*, p. 84.

[168]. VILLEY Michel, *Le droit romain* Que sais-je?, n° 195, PUF, p. 12.

[169]. POTHIER, *Oeuvres*, Paris, 1847, book IX, *Traité du domaine de propriété*, p. 186, n° 245.

[170]. TZITZIS Stamatios, *Esthétique de la Violence*, Paris, PUF, 1997, p. 100, translated from French: "Au coeur du droit, réside le respect de la propriété. On ne peut être maître que de ce qu'on possède".

[171]. *Cf.* previous note n° 9 Karl JASPERS's definition of the axial period.

[172]. According to Michel VILLEY, they do not sufficiently take into account the Greek philosophy which should allow a better understanding of the classical Roman Law. Michel VILLEY, *Suum jus cuique tribuens*, Milano, Giuffré, 1954.

[173]. REVILLOUT Eugène, *Les origines égyptiennes du droit civil romain*, Librairie Paul Geuthner, paris, 1912.

[174]. HUVELIN Paul, *Les tablettes magiques et le droit romain*, Macon, Protat Frères, 1901.

[175]. For sure received from the Egyptians but also improved by the Romans.

[176]. On the pragmatism of the ancient Roman lawyers, *cf.* Pierangelo CATALANO, *Diritto e Personne, Studi su origine e attualità del sistema romano*, G. GIPAIICHELLI EDITORE, Torino, 1990, p. XIII.

[177]. On Roman Law as the art of sharing, VILLEY Michel, *Le Droit Romain, op. cit.,* p. 116; presentation by Michel VILLEY of Emmanuel KANT's work, *Métaphysique des moeurs, Première partie, Doctrine du Droit*, Vrin, Paris, 1993, p. 20; Michel VILLEY, *Suum jus cuique tribuens*, Milano, Giuffré, 1954, p. 365.

[178]. Due to the specific geography of Egypt, this people has been particularly dependent on nature and especially on the inundation of the Nile. Hence the great attention they paid to nature.

[179]. AMÉLINEAU Emile, *La morale égyptienne quinze siècles avant notre ère, Etude sur le papyrus de Boulaq n° 4*, Paris, Editions Ernest Leroux, 1892, p. LV.

[180]. GOFF Beatrice L., *Symbols Of Ancient Egypt In The Late Period, The Twenty-first Dynasty*, Yale University, Mouton publishers, 1979, p. 19.

[181]. LÉVY-BRUHL Henri, *Nouvelles Etudes sur le Très Ancien Droit romain*, Paris, Recueil Sirey, 1947, p. 6, HUVELIN Paul, *Les tablettes magiques et le droit romain*, Macon, Protat Frères, 1901, p. 42 and note 1, p. 10, p. 11.

[182]. LÉVY-BRUHL Henri, *Nouvelles Etudes sur le Très Ancien Droit romain*, Paris, Recueil Sirey, 1947, p. 6, HUVELIN Paul, *Les tablettes magiques et le droit romain*, Macon, Protat Frères, 1901, p. 11.

[183]. VILLEY Michel, *Le Droit Romain, op. cit.*, p. 80.

[184]. On the distortion of the ancient Roman Law *cf.* VILLEY Michel, "Métamorphoses de l'obligation", Archives de philosophie du droit, *op. cit.*, p. 288; VILLEY Michel, "La notion romaine classique de *Jus* et le *Dikaion* d'Aristote", La filosofia greca e il diritto romano, Roma, Accademia Nazionale dei Lincei, 1976, pp. 71-79, p. 76.

[185]. On the opinion that there are no legal gaps regarding the Internet *cf.* previous note n° 120.

[186]. On the difficulty met in the field of copyright in trying to apply an international law built upon the concept of territory, *cf. The Future Of Copyright In A Digital Environment*, editor P. Bernt HUGENHOLTZ, Proceedings of the Royal Academy Colloquium, Amsterdam, 6-7 July 1995, KLUWER LAW INTERNATIONAL, The hague, London, Boston, 1996.

187. SéDALLIAN Valérie, *Droit de l'Internet*, Paris, Net Press, collection AUI, 1997; ITEANU Olivier, *Internet et le droit, Aspect juridiques du commerce électronique*, Paris, Eyrolles, 1996; BRESSE Pierre, KAUFMAN Gautier, *Guide juridique de l'internet et du commerce électronique*, Paris, Vuibert, 2000; *Internet, Aspects juridiques*, under the direction of Alain BENSOUSSAN, Paris, Hermès, 1996; *Internet saisi par le Droit*, Travaux de l'A.F.D.I.T., under the direction of Xavier LINANT de BELLEFONDS, Paris, Editions des Parques, 1997; PIETTE-COUDOL Thierry, *Internet et la loi*, Paris, Dalloz, 1997; GRINGAS Clive, *The Laws of the Internet*, London, Butterworths, 1997; TRUDEL Pierre, ABRAN France, BENYEKHIEF Karin, HEIN Sophie, *Droit du Cyberespace*, Montréal, Thémis, Paris, 1998.

188. On the French will to control and stamp web sites, *cf.* LORENTZ Francis, *La nouvelle donne du commerce électronique: réalisations 1998 et perspectives: rapport de la mission Commerce électronique*, France, Ministère de l'économie, des finances et de l'industrie, Paris, Editions de Bercy, Etudes ISSN 1245-2246, 1999, II.2.4. But as CORDIER's report states: "The French law is the most demanding, but only 5 % web sites are French" (translated from French: "La loi française est la plus exigeante, mais seuls 5 % des sites sont français".), Sénat, *Rapport Cordier, Rapport de la Commission de réflexion sur le livre numérique*, May 1999. http://www.culture.gouv.fr/culture/actualites/rapports/cordier/edition.htm#

189. *Cf.* LESSIG Lawrence, *Code And Other Laws Of Cyberspace*, Basic Books, NY, 1999; Marc STEFIK, *The Internet Edge, Social, Legal and Technological Challenges for a Networked World*, MIT, 1999.

190. VILLEY Michel, in the presentation of the work of Immanuel KANT, *Métaphysique des moeurs, Première partie, Doctrine du Droit*, Paris, Vrin, 1993, p. 23; HERVADA Javier, *Introduction critique au droit naturel*, Bordeaux, EDITIONS BIERE, 1991, p. 43, p. 51, p. 86; Aristote, *Ethique à Nicomaque*, translation J. TRICOT, Paris, VRIN, 1983, p. 224 and pp. 245-246.

191. MATHIAS Paul, *La cité Internet*, Paris, Presses de Sciences PO, La bibliothèque du citoyen, 1997, pp. 72-73. *Cf.* also against censorship over the Internet:
- Citizens Internet Empowerment Coalition http://www.ciec.org/,
- Peacefire: http://www.peacefire.org/,
- XEMU Censorship Web-page: http://www.xemu.demon.co.uk/censor/index.html.

192. This is also Michel VILLEY's opinion in "La notion romaine classique de *Jus* et le *Dikaion* d'Aristote", *La filosofia greca e il diritto romano*, Roma, Accademia Nazionale dei Lincei, 1976, pp. 71-79, p. 73.

193. An agricultural and materialistic world.

194. *Cf.* ARISTOTLE, *Ethique à Nicomaque*, translation by J. TRICOT, VRIN, Paris, 1983, p. 224 and pp. 245-246; VILLEY Michel, "La notion

romaine classique de *Jus* et le *Dikaion* d'Aristote", *La filosofia greca e il diritto romano*, Roma, Accademia Nazionale dei Lincei, 1976, pp. 71-79, p. 73.

195. RAWLS John, *Théorie de la justice*, Paris, Seuil, Point Essais, translated from Engligh by Catherine AUDARD, p. 33.

196. Lawyers are pitifully innovative, *cf.* for example: GAUTIER Pierre-Yves, "Philosophie du droit d'auteur 'on line'", pp. 133-145, in *Internet saisi par le Droit*, Paris, Travaux de l'A.F.D.I.T., under the direction of direction de Xavier LINANT de BELLEFONDS, Paris, Editions des Parques, 1997. ITEANU Olivier *Internet et le droit, Aspect juridiques du commerce électronique*, Paris, Eyrolles, 1996, p. 8. The French Conseil d'Etat which was charged by the Prime Minister to study the legal changes made necessary by the Internet reached the conclusion that the very foundations of French law is not undermined. Conseil d'Etat, France, *op. cit.*, 2 July 1998, Paris, La Documentation française, 1998, synthèse.

197. *Cf.: Which Court Decides? Which Law Applies? Quel tribunal décide? Quel droit s'applique?*, Edited by/under the direction of Katharina BOELE-WOELKI and Catherine KESSEDJIAN, Kluwer Law International, The hague, London, Boston, 1998, Proceedings of the international colloquium in honour of Michel PELICHET organized by the Molengraaff Institute of Private Law, University of Utrecht and the Hague Conference on Private International Law.

198. While in Babylon the Hammurabi Code received from the sun-god, *cf.* Joseph SARRAF, *op. cit.*, p. 31.

199. *Cf.* LALOUETTE Claire, *Textes sacrés et Textes profanes de l'Ancienne Egypte, book II: Mythes, contes et poésies*, Paris, Gallimard/Unesco, 1987, p. 84: about the first International treaty, dated 1278 B.C, Between Rameses II and Hattusili III.

200. *Ibid*, Joseph SARRAF, introduction.

201. From the present knowledge in the field of Egyptology we know that the weighing of the souls has become individual around 2000 B.C. Before that time it was reserved for the King.

202. ASSMANN Jan, *Maât, l'Egypte pharaonique et l'idée de justice sociale, op. cit.*, p. 13.

203. HORNUNG Erik, *L'esprit du temps des pharaons*, Hachette, *op. cit.*, p. 137.

204. That is to say the social, the religious, the cosmic, etc.

205. RACHET Guy, *Le livre des morts des anciens Égyptiens, op. cit.*, p. 141.

206. According to Claire LALOUETTE, *Textes sacrés et Textes profanes de l'Ancienne Egypte*, book I: *op. cit.*, p. 84, translated from French: « Maât est la force de Rê, l'élue de Rê ».

[207].RACHET Guy, *Le livre des morts des anciens Égyptiens*, *op. cit.,* p. 174: "Je suis le maître de la lumière". (I am the master of light), p. 180 on light.

[208]. Guy RACHET, *Le livre des morts des anciens Égyptiens*, Editions du Rocher, 1996, p. 163.

[209]. *Cf.* "L'homme de l'Oasis" ("The peasant"), translation by Claire LALOUETTE, *Textes sacrés et Textes profanes de l'Ancienne Egypte*, book I: *Des Pharaons et des Hommes*, *op. cit.*, p. 203.

[210]. On the meaning of "righteous" and on the consequences of being in conformity with Maat, *cf.* FRANKFORT Henri, *Ancient Egyptian Religion, An Interpretation*, *op. cit.*, p. 72; *cf.* MORENZ Siegfried, *Egyptian Religion*, *op. cit.*, pp. 113-116.

[211]. LALOUETTE Claire, *Textes sacrés et Textes profanes de l'Ancienne Egypte, book II: Mythes, contes et poésies*, *op. cit.*, p. 32.

[212]. RACHET Guy, *Le livre des morts des anciens Égyptiens*, Editions du Rocher, 1996, p. 173-174 and p. 173.

[213]. On Maat and Isfet, *cf.* LICHTHEIM Myriam, *op. cit.*, p. 18.

[214].RACHET Guy, *Le livre des morts des anciens Égyptiens*, *op. cit.*, p. 173-174 and p. 173.

[215]. YOYOTTE Jean, "Le jugement des morts selon l'Egypte ancienne", *op. cit.,* p. 21.

[216]. YOYOTTE Jean, "La pensée préphilosophique en Egypte", *op. cit.*, p. 1-23; p. 11.

[217]. FRANKFORT Henri, *Ancient Egyptian Religion, An Interpretation*, *op. cit.*, p. 132.

[218]. HORNUNG Erik, *L'esprit du temps des pharaons*, *op. cit.*, p. 99. Compare with "La prophéthie de Neferty" ("the Prophecy of Neferti"), translated by LALOUETTE Claire, *Textes sacrés et Textes profanes de l'Ancienne Egypte*, book I: *Des Pharaons et des Hommes*, *op. cit.*, p. 71.

[219]. HORNUNG Erik, *L'esprit du temps des pharaons*, *op. cit., p.* 139.

[220]. LALOUETTE Claire, *Textes sacrés et Textes profanes de l'Ancienne Egypte, book II: Mythes, contes et poésies*, *op. cit.*, p. 14.

[221].RACHET Guy, *Le livre des morts des anciens Égyptiens*, *op. cit.*, p. 145; compare with FAULKNER Raymond, *The Ancient Egyptian Book Of The Dead*, British Museum Press, London, 1996, p. 79.

[222].RACHET Guy, *Le livre des morts des anciens Égyptiens*, *op. cit.*, p. 151.

[223].RACHET Guy, *Le livre des morts des anciens Égyptiens*, *op. cit.*, p. 149.

[224]. RACHET Guy, *Le livre des morts des anciens Égyptiens*, *op. cit.*, p. 151.

[225]. Guy RACHET, *Le livre des morts des anciens Égyptiens*, *op. cit.*, p. 141.

[226]. RACHET Guy, *Le livre des morts des anciens Égyptiens*, *op. cit.*

[227]. "L'art de Vivre du Vizir Ptahhotep", translation by Claire LALOUETTE, *Textes sacrés et Textes profanes de l'Ancienne Egypte*, book I: *Des Pharaons et des Hommes*, *op. cit.*, p. 241.

[228]. *Cf.* "Les deux serpents du rêve de TANOUTAMON et la conquête de l'Egypte", translation by LALOUETTE Claire, *Textes sacrés et Textes profanes de l'Ancienne Egypte*, book I: *Des Pharaons et des Hommes*, *op. cit.*, p. 42.

[229]. L'art de vivre du vizir PTAHHOTEP", translation by Claire LALOUETTE, *Textes sacrés et Textes profanes de l'Ancienne Egypte*, book I: *Des Pharaons et des Hommes*, *op. cit.*, p. 239.

[230]. *Cf.* "Le grand-prêtre PETOSIRIS et sa famille (vers 360 av. JC)", translation by Claire LALOUETTE, *Textes sacrés et Textes profanes de l'Ancienne Egypte*, book I: *Des Pharaons et des Hommes*, 1984, Gallimard/Unesco, p. 262. *Cf.* on the heart as a guide, Myriam LICHTHEIM, *op. cit.*, p. 53.

[231]. "L'art de Vivre du Vizir PTAHHOTEP", translation by Claire LALOUETTE, *Textes sacrés et Textes profanes de l'Ancienne Egypte*, book I: *Des Pharaons et des Hommes*, 1984, Gallimard/Unesco, p. 236; and book 2, p. 49.

[232]. *Cf.* "Les chants du désespéré XIIe dynastie dialogue entre l'homme et son ba", translation by Claire LALOUETTE, *Textes sacrés et Textes profanes de l'Ancienne Egypte*, book I: *Des Pharaons et des Hommes*, *op. cit.*, p. 222.

[233]. RACHET Guy, *Le livre des morts des anciens Egyptiens*, *op. cit.*, p. 61.

[234]. *Cf.* "l'enseignement du roi AMENEMHAT I à son fils SESOSTRIS", translation by Claire LALOUETTE, *Textes sacrés et Textes profanes de l'Ancienne Egypte*, book I: Des Pharaons et des Hommes, 1984, Gallimard/Unesco, p. 57.

[235]. *Cf.* "Les lamentations d'IPOU-OUR", translation by Claire LALOUETTE, *Textes sacrés et Textes profanes de l'Ancienne Egypte*, book I: *op. cit.*, p. 215.

[236]. *Cf.* a book totally dedicated to this subject: PIANKOFF Alexandre, *Le "coeur" dans les textes égyptiens*, Paris, Librairie Paul Geuthner, 1930.

[237]. "Le décret D'HOREMHEB 1340 av. JC", translation by LALOUETTE Claire, *Textes sacrés et Textes profanes de l'Ancienne Egypte*, book I: *Des Pharaons et des Hommes, op. cit.*, p. 83.

[238]. SHUPAK Nili, "Some Idioms Connected With The Concept Of 'Heart'", in *Egypt And The Bible, Pharaonic Egypt, The Bible And Christianity*, Jerusalem, Edition. S. Israelit-Groll, the Magnes Press, The Hebrew University, 1985, 202-212, p. 203 on the link between ears and the heart.

[239]. HORNUNG Erik, *L'esprit du temps des pharaons, op. cit.*, p. 134.

[240]. "La prophétie de Neferty", translation by LALOUETTE Claire, *Textes sacrés et Textes profanes de l'Ancienne Egypte*, book I: *Des Pharaons et des Hommes, op. cit.*, p. 71.

[241]. RACHET Guy, *Le livre des morts des anciens Égyptiens, op. cit.*, p. 141; 149. *Cf.* also: "Textes sculptés sur les parois d'une des chapelles de TOUTANKHAMON qui régna vers 1350 av. J,-C ", translated by LALOUETTE Claire, textes sacrés, book 1, *op. cit.*. p. 155 and same author same book p. 179: "Les exploits valeureux du commandant AMENEMHEB (vers 1480- 1440 av. J.-C.)".

[242]. RACHET Guy, *Le livre des morts des anciens Égyptiens, op. cit.*, pp. 162-16; *cf.* also: "les Enseignements de PTAHOTEP", translation by LALOUETTE Claire, *Textes sacrés et Textes profanes de l'Ancienne Egypte*, book I: *Des Pharaons et des Hommes*, 1984, Gallimard/Unesco, p. 265.

[243]. Which is a simple use of the principle of passage or not of an energy through a material thing.

[244]. RACHET Guy, *Le livre des morts des anciens Égyptiens, op. cit.*, p. 161.

[245]. RACHET Guy, *Le livre des morts des anciens Égyptiens, op. cit.*, p. 161.

[246]. "La satire des métiers", translation by Claire LALOUETTE, *Textes sacrés et Textes profanes de l'Ancienne Egypte*, book I: *Des Pharaons et des Hommes, op. cit.*, p. 197; *cf.* also "L'homme de l'Oasis", *ibid*, p. 203; *ibid.*, p. 255 "l'enseignement du scribe ANI."

[247]. *Cf.* PIERRET, *Etudes Egyptologiques*, II, p. 94 and following, quoted by MORET Alexandre, "Rituel du culte divin en Egypte", p. 149, note, n° 1.

[248]. We can find it in the *Book Of The Dead* regarding the deceased and in many texts regarding the Kings. *Cf.* for example: Claire LALOUETTE, *Textes sacrés et Textes profanes de l'Ancienne Egypte*, book I: *Des Pharaons et des Hommes*, 1984, Gallimard/Unesco, p. 153 and p. 179.

[249]. LALOUETTE Claire, Textes sacrés et Textes profanes de l'Ancienne Egypte, *book II: Mythes, contes et poésies*, 1987, *op. cit.*, p. 27.

[250]. "L'homme de l'Oasis", translation by Claire LALOUETTE, *Textes sacrés et Textes profanes de l'Ancienne Egypte*, book I: *Des Pharaons et des Hommes*, 1984, Gallimard/Unesco, p. 204; and *ibid* p. 208, p. 209 *Cf.* LICHTHEIM Myriam, *op. cit.*, p. 59 "I abominate rapacity" and p. 61: "I am truly straight, free of greed."

[251]. On the lack of the concept of sin in Ancient Egypt: *cf.* FRANKFORT Henri, *Ancient Egyptian Religion, An Interpretation*, *op. cit.*, p. 73.

[252]. LALOUETTE Claire, *Textes sacrés et Textes profanes de l'Ancienne Egypte*, book 1 *op. cit.*, p. 210.

[253]. *Cf.* Ani's papyrus, translated par Guy RACHET, *Le livre des morts des anciens Égyptiens*, *op. cit.*, p. 193.

[254]. "L'homme de l'Oasis", translation by Claire LALOUETTE, *Textes sacrés et Textes profanes de l'Ancienne Egypte*, book I: *Des Pharaons et des Hommes*, *op. cit.*, p. 204.

[255]. "l'homme de l'Oasis", translation by Claire LALOUETTE, *Textes sacrés et Textes profanes de l'Ancienne Egypte*, book I: *Des Pharaons et des Hommes*, 1984, Gallimard/Unesco, p. 205.

[256]. "L'instruction royaliste de SEHETEPIBREÊ", translation by Claire LALOUETTE, *Textes sacrés et Textes profanes de l'Ancienne Egypte*, book I: *Des Pharaons et des Hommes*, 1984, Gallimard/Unesco, p. 75.

[257]. RACHET Guy, *Le livre des morts des anciens Égyptiens*, *op. cit.*, p. 141.

[258]. RACHET Guy, *Le livre des morts des anciens Égyptiens*, *op. cit.*, p. 86.

[259]. It is also stated that it is linked to the free flow of the water of the Nile, during the inundations. But these last are also due to a cosmic phenomenon as the Sirius star announces the Nile inundations. On this cosmic phenomenon, *Cf.* WILSON Hilary, *Understanding Hieroglyphs*, London, Brockhampton Press, 1999, p. 174.

[260]. SHIRUN-GRUMACH Irene, "Remarks On The Goddess MAAT", *Pharaonic Egypt, The Bible And Christianity*, *op. cit.*, p. 173 on the feather, Maat, and the light.

[261]. *Op. cit.*, p. 29 and note 10, translated from French "Puisse-t-il vivre, être en bonne santé et prospérer". *Cf.* also LICHTHEIM Myriam, *op. cit.*, p. 27 "life, prosperity, health!".

[262]. Translation by Claire LALOUETTE, *Textes sacrés et Textes profanes de l'Ancienne Egypte*, book I: *Des Pharaons et des Hommes*,

Anna Mancini

1984, Gallimard/Unesco p. 29, p. 33, p. 67, p. 239, p. 258, and p. 75: "Enseignements à Mérikarê".

263. As an example, *cf.* LICHTHEIM Myriam, *op. cit.,* p. 35: "I am a hearer who hears the truth, I am exact like the balance, truly straight like Thoth". On filling the ears with Maat, *cf.* LICHTHEIM Myriam, *op. cit.,* p. 50: "Who fills the ears of Horus with truth".

264. On justice as the art of sharing *cf.* previous note n° 199.

265. This one also operates in the traditional world but on a lower level.

266. MAUSS Marcel, "Essai sur le don", *op. cit.,* p. 157, p. 159, especially p. 161.

267. MAUSS Marcel, "Essai sur le don", *op. cit.,* p. 160.

268. MAUSS Marcel, "Essai sur le don", *op. cit.,* p. 165.

269. MAUSS Marcel, "Essai sur le don", *op. cit.,* p. 180.

270. Marcel MAUSS, "Essai sur le don", *op. cit.,* p. 176.

271. BLEIBERG Edward, *The Official Gift In Ancient Egypt*, Oklahoma, University of Oklahoma Press., 1996.

272. BLEIBERG Edward, *op. cit.,* p. 7.

273. BLEIBERG Edward, *op. cit.,* p. 5.

274. BLEIBERG Edward, *op. cit.,* p. 27.

275. BLEIBERG Edward, *op. cit.,* p. 27.

276. BLEIBERG Edward, *op. cit.,* p. 23.

277. MAUSS Marcel, "Essai sur le don", *op. cit.,* p. 151.

278. "L'échange est au coeur de la civilisation égyptienne", Entretien avec Jean YOYOTTE, *Eurêka*, BAYARD PRESSE, Paris, September 1998, n° 35, translated from French: "L'échange est au coeur de la civilization égyptienne" and "que toute la société égyptienne s'inscrit dans le cadre d'un échange entre les dieux et les humains."

279. GOYON Jean-Claude, *Maât et Pharaon ou de destin de l'Egypte antique, op. cit.,* p. 85.

280. Lionel THOUMYRE, *Abuses In The Cyberspace, The Regulation Of Illicit Messages Diffused On The Internet*, Thesis, CRID Namur, Belgium, 1996, http://www.juriscom.net.

281. I give in order that you give, and "primitive people said: "If I give to gods, I receive much more".

282. *Cf.* on the effect of Netscape on the development of the Internet, QUITTNER Joshua & SLATALLA Michelle, *Speeding The Net*, London, Orion Business Books, 1998.

154

[283]. Compare with LORENTZ's report, *op. cit.,* which is opposite to the dynamics of the Internet when proposing a control of the registration with browsers. The excuse is consumers protection, V.5.1

[284]. *Cf.* Serge GUÉRIN, *Internet en questions*, Economica, Paris, 1997, p. 87.

[285]. We do not need to be physically wealthy in order to be able to give in the virtual world. When giving in the virtual world we do not become poorer, it is the opposite which normally occurs.

[286]. Which tends to generate profits thanks to scarcity associated with the great economic law of offer and demand. This law is true in the physical world by essence limited, but false within the Internet.

[287]. That is to say that they can do the same with other existing means. In this case the Internet is one more means which does not change the principle of their action.

[288]. Lionel THOUMYRE, *op. cit.,* Thesis, CRID Namur, Belgium, 1996, http://www.juriscom.net.

[289]. At the beginning it was a space of freedom self-regulated through the "Netiquette".

[290]. *Cf.* Rapport LORENTZ, *op. cit.,* III.2.4. On the will to fight against undesirable contents and III.5.12 on the will to protect consumers. *Cf.* Conseil d'Etat, France, *Internet et les réseaux numériques, étude adoptée par l'Assemblée générale du Conseil d'Etat le 2 July 1998*, Paris, La Documentation française, 1998, recommandation n° 1, 2 et 4.

[291]. The risk of decrease in tax income is one of the major fear of states with regard to the Internet, *cf.* LORENTZ's report, *op. cit.,* III.2.

[292]. This attitude is particularly strong in France where a will to control the "quality" of the web sites has been manifested, *cf.* Rapport LORENTZ, *op. cit.,* II.2.4.

[293]. *Cf.* in the same line: GRAHAM Gordon, *The Internet:// A Philosophical Inquiry*, NY, Routledge, 1999, p. 118: "Now it can be argued with respect to some media that ignoring pornographic material is easier said than done. Billboards and public broadcasting stations intrude upon the public willy-nilly (or at least they can) and sometimes this is true of book stalls also. Let us agree that this is so, but if it is, it makes pornography on the Internet of less concern than pornography elsewhere. There may be a vast amount of pornographic material there if I choose to surf for it, but if I choose not to, my senses and sensibilities will remain unscathed."
This is also the case with the Minitel "messageries roses" (chat lines).

[294]. Paul MATHIAS, in his book *La cité Internet*, Paris, Presses de Sciences PO, La bibliothèque du citoyen, 1997, pp. 72-73, speaks about governments legal hysteria with regard to the Internet.

[295]. *Cf.* Ira MAGAZINER, *Framework For Global Electronic Commerce*, 1st July 1997, http://www.ecommerce.gov/: "... governments must adopt a non-regulatory, market-oriented approach to electronic commerce, one that facilitates the emergence of a transparent and predictable legal environment to support global business and commerce. Official decision makers must respect the unique nature of the medium and recognize that widespread competition and increased consumer choice should be the defining features of the new digital marketplace". For an analysis of the American position by France, *cf.* Francis LORENTZ, *La nouvelle donne du commerce électronique: réalisations 1998 et perspectives: rapport de la mission Commerce électronique*, France, Ministère de l'économie, des finances et de l'industrie, Paris, Editions de Bercy, Etudes ISSN 1245-2246, 1999, II.1. "Une initiative américaine: supprimer les barrières au commerce électronique." http://www.telecom.gouv.fr/francais/activ/techno/techndoc/technodoc.ht m

[296]. Reno v. ACLU, 26 June 1997, n° 96-511:
http://www.aclu.org/issues/cyber/trial/sctran.html
Communications Decency act, text:http://www.epic.org/cda/cda;
Decision and other documents: http://www.epic.org/cda.

[297]. EPIC web site: http://www.epic.org.

[298]. In the field of intellectual property, an author underlined the difficulty met by states in exercising their sovereignty, VERHOEVEN Joe, "Souveraineté et mondialisation: libres propos", in La mondialisation du droit, under the direction of Eric LOQUIN and Catherine KESSEDJIAN, Travaux du Centre de Recherche sur le droit des marchés et des investissements internationaux, book 19, LITEC, 2000, pp. 43-57, p. 51.

[299]. Which is not the case in France which by its attitude endangers the balance of the international relations. In effect, France wants to fight actively against the undesirable contents available on the Internet. According to the report of the French Conseil d'Etat, *op. cit.*, 1998, p. 129, the French criminal law must be applied regarding undesirable messages available on the Internet, wherever they come from, insofar as, when received by French people they become a forming element of an offence. We believe such a position to be a very bad example for other countries. What about if this example were followed by all the other countries of the Globe? This does not prevent French courts to go on fighting in this way. Recently Yahoo USA has been asked by the Tribunal de Grande Instance of Paris to take action in order to stop the flow through its servers of information illegal in France, but not in the United States, *cf.* Le Figaro, mardi 25 July 2000, p. 5.
In another field, regarding PINOCHET's affair, an author underlines the dangerous tendency of states to try to exert their coercive powers outside their respective territories: VERHOEVEN Joe, "Souveraineté et mondialisation: libres propos", *La mondialisation du droit,* under the direction of Eric LOQUIN and Catherine KESSEDJIAN, Travaux du Centre

de Recherche sur le droit des marchés et des investissements internationaux, book 19, LITEC, 2000, *op. cit.,* p. 54.

[300]. Even the creation of a coercive international set of laws, proposed by Joe VERHOEVEN, will not allow to solve this question. VERHOEVEN Joe, "Souveraineté et mondialisation: libres propos", *op. cit.,* pp. 43-57, p. 55.

[301]. Court TV:
http://www.courttv.com/old/library/cyberlaw/ny_decency.html

[302]. Such a phenomenon also occurred with the Minitel. A movement against the "Minitel Rose" (adult services) resulted in a decrease in the Minitel use. Therefore France Télécom had to launch an advertising campaign to renew the Minitel image and to encourage its use. Moreover, on another ground, an author notices that all what is forbidden is made more attractive: Gordon GRAHAM, *The Internet:// A Philosophical Inquiry*, NY, Routledge, 1999, p. 124.

[303]. On another ground, we can mention the example of the French government which shows an active will to "purify" the Internet while the French Minitel is far from be "pure".

[304]. Or they should totally forbid access to the Internet.

[305]. This has been underlined several times by the French Conseil d'Etat, France, *op. cit.,* 2 July 1998, Paris, La Documentation française, 1998, *passim.*

[306]. This risk has been noticed by the French Conseil d'Etat, Conseil d'Etat, France, *op. cit.,* p. 76 and p. 78.

[307]. The Minitel was lent to the users.

[308]. On the Minitel technical aspects *cf.*: RINCE Jean-Yves, *Le Minitel*, Paris, PUF, Que Sais-je?, n° 2539, 1990, p. 13; on online services *cf*: BRETON Thierry, *Les téléservices en France*, Paris, la Documentation française, 1994; for an economic analysis of the Minitel, see: OECD, *France's experience with the Minitel: lessons for electronic commerce over the Internet*, DSTI/ICCP/ie (97) 10/FINAL, http://www.ocde.org.

[309]. This company was totally State-owned, when in charge of launching the Minitel.

[310]. *C.f.* OECD, *op. cit.*, p. 19.

[311]. Much greater than the wealth permitted by the abusive use of the Minitel.

[312]. Nevertheless France Télécom has now allowed a worldwide access to the French Minitel through the Internet, and which still uses the kiosk system.

[313]. OECD, *op. cit.*, p. 23.

[314]. French people had not yet access to the Internet.

[315]. Still effective though the extension of the Internet use in France.

[316]. On the tariff *cf.* http://www.francetélécom.fr.

[317]. According to Guy LACROIX, *Le mirage Internet, enjeux économiques et sociaux, op. cit., p.* 124, at the beginning France Télécom retained half of the price of the service, then in 1997 it retained from 30 to 50 % according to the services.

[318]. Still effective though the extention of the Internet use in France.

[319]. OECD, *op. cit.*, p. 22.

[320]. Especially the enrichment of the providers of "adult services". It has been proved that the Minitel could initially boom thanks to the significant part of the market constituted by "adult services". Which did not seem to embarrass the French public authorities. Moreover, as the French State had a total power on the Minitel, it was able to stop selectively the flow of this kind of information without hindering the whole information flow. Thanks to France Télécom, the adult lines of the Minitel are now accessible worldwide through the Internet. Which is stricking as France is manifesting a strong will to "purify" the Internet.

[321]. French National Railways company, (Société Française des Chemins de Fer Français).

[322]. One just needed to pay to France Télécom the price for a local call.

[323]. The SNCF data is now available on the Internet for the price of local calls.

[324]. 2,23 F (about 0,31 USD) per minute.

[325]. This, notwithstanding its monopolistic position.

[326]. As it is now the case with the Internet, *cf.,* revue *France TGV*, Paris, septembre 2000, n° 27, p. 16.

[327]. Generally speaking that is to say persons but also goods.

158

BIBLIOGRAPHY

INTERNET LAW: ARTICLES, BOOKS AND REPORTS

AFTEL, *Internet: les enjeux pour la France: Livre blanc*, Puteaux, 1996

AFTEL, *Le droit du multimédia: de la télématique à Internet, Paris Ed. du Téléphone*, 1996

BAPTISTE Eric, *L'infosphère: stratégies des médias et rôle de l'Etat*, 1er mars 2000 http://www.telecom.gouv.fr/francais/activ/techno/techndoc/technodoc. htm

BELLEFONDS Xavier LINANT de, under the direction of, *Internet saisi par le Droit*, Travaux de l'A.F.D.I.T., Paris, Editions des Parques, 1997

BENSOUSSAN Alain, under the direction of: *Internet, Aspects juridiques,* Paris, Hermès, 1996

BOELE-WOELKI Katharina and KESSEDJIAN Catherine Edited by/under the direction of, *Which Court Decides? Which Law Applies? Quel tribunal décide? Quel droit s'applique?,* The hague, London, Boston, Kluwer Law International, 1998, Proceedings of the international colloquium in honour of Michel PELICHET organized by the Molengraaff Institute of Private Law, University of Utrecht and the Hague Conference on Private International Law

BRESSE Pierre, KAUFMAN Gautier, *Guide juridique de l'internet et du commerce électronique*, Paris, Vuibert, 2000

Conseil d'Etat, France, *Internet et les réseaux numériques, étude adoptée par l'Assemblée générale du Conseil d'Etat le 2 juillet 1998*, Paris, La Documentation française, 1998

DEPREZ Pierre, FAUCHOUX Vincent, *Lois, contrats et usages du multimédia*, Paris, Dixit, 1997

FALQUE-PIERROTIN Isabelle, *Internet: enjeux juridiques*, France Mission interministérielle sur l'internet, Paris, La Documentaiton française, Collection des rapports officiels, 1997 http://www.telecom.gouv.fr/francais/activ/techno/techndoc/technodoc. htm

France, Premier Ministre, *Préparer l'entrée de la France dans la société de l'information: programme d'action gouvernemental*, Paris, La Documentation française, 1998 http://www.premier-ministre.gouv.fr http://www.admifrance.gouv.fr

France, Service juridique et technique de l'information, *La France dans la société de l'information*, La documentation française, 1999

GELLER Paul Edward, "Conflicts of law in cyberspace: International copyright in a digitally networked world", in *The Future Of Copyright In A Digital Environment*, Editor P. Bernt HUGENHOLTZ, Proceedings of the Royal Academy Colloquium, Amsterdam, 6-7 July 1995, The hague, London, Boston, KLUWER LAW INTERNATIONAL, 1996, pp. 27-48

GRINGAS Clive, *The Laws Of The Internet*, London, Butterworths, 1997

HUET Jérôme, *Droit de l'informatique et des télécommunications*, Paris, Litec, 1991

ITEANU Olivier, *Internet et le droit, Aspect juridiques du commerce électronique*, Paris, Eyrolles, 1996

LORENTZ Francis, *La nouvelle donne du commerce électronique: réalisations 1998 et perspectives: rapport de la mission Commerce électronique*, France, Ministère de l'économie, des finances et de l'industrie, Paris, Èditions de Bercy, Etudes ISSN 1245-2246, 1999. http://www.telecom.gouv.fr/francais/activ/techno/techndoc/technodoc. htm

MAGAZINER Ira, The White House, CLINTON Bill, AL GORE, *Framework For Global Electronic Commerce*, July 1997, http://www.ecommerce.gov/

MARTIN Jean, "Le cyberespace: un prétendu vide juridique", Le Monde, 3 mai 1996

MARTIN-LALANDE Patrice, *L'Internet: un vrai défi pour la France*; rapport au Premier Ministre, Paris, la Documentation française, 1998

MILEO Thierry, Commissariat Général du Plan, *Les réseaux de la société de l'Information*, Paris, Editions ESKA, 1996

PAUL Christian, *Du droit et des libertés sur l'internet*, juin 2000, http://www.internet.gouv.fr/rapportcpaul.htm

PIETTE-COUDOL Thierry, *Internet et la loi*, Paris, Dalloz, 1997

SéDALLIAN Valérie, *Droit de l'Internet*, Paris, Net Press, collection AUI, 1997 (AUI: Association des Utilisateurs d'Internet. http://www.aui.fr)

SMITH Graham JH, Edited by, *Internet Law and Regulation*, Bird & Bird, London, Second edition, Published by FT Law & Tax, 1997

THOUMYRE Lionel, *Abuses In The Cyberspace, The Regulation Of Illicit Messages Diffused On The Internet*, Thesis, CRID Namur, Belgium, 1996, http://www.juriscom.net

TOSI, Emilio, *I problemi giuridici di Internet*, Milano, Giuffrè, 1999

TRUDEL Pierre, ABRAN France, BENYEKHIEF Karin, HEIN Sophie, *Droit du Cyberespace*, Montréal, Thémis, 1998

VIVANT Michel, *Les créations immatérielles et le droit*, Paris, Ellipses, 1997, CNRS

THINKING ON THE INTERNET AND ON THE MINITEL

ABADIE Michel, *Minitel Story*, Paris, Publi S.A., 1988

BALLE Francis, *Médias et Sociétés, de Gutenberg à Internet*, Paris, Montchrestien, 1997

BRETON Thierry, *Les téléservices en France*, Paris, la Documentation française, 1994

BROWN Geoffrey, *The Information Game, Ethical Issues In A Microchip, World*, NJ and London, Humanities Press International,1990

CACOMO, Jean-Louis, *Les défis économiques de l'information*, Paris, L'harmattan, 1996

CARNOI Martin, CASTELLS Manuel, COHEN Stephen S., CARDOSO Fernando Henrique, *The New Global Economy In The Information Age*, The Pensylvania State University Press, The MACMILLAN PRESS LTD, 1993

CREMOC, Centre de recherche sur l'Europe et le monde contemporain, *La Galaxie internet, l'impératif de la conquête: ouvrage réalisé d'après les travaux effectués lors du colloque "Internet, un outil stratégique pour les Etats et les Entreprises"*, Paris. Unicomm, Les cahiers du CREMOC, 1999

DAVIDSON James Dale and REES-MOGG William, *The Sovereign Individual, The Coming Economic Revolution*, London, MACMILLAN, 1997

FREEMAN J. DYSON, *The sun, the genome, the internet, Tools of Scientific Revolutions*, NY, Oxford University Press, 1999

GATES Bill, *Business @ The Speed Of Thought*, London, Penguin Books, 1999

GRAHAM Gordon, *The Internet:// A Philosophical Inquiry*, NY, Routledge, 1999

GUÉRIN Serge, *Internet en questions*, Paris, Economica, 1997

GUILLAUME Marc (under the direction of), *Où vont les autoroutes de l'information*, Commissariat Général du Plan, Commission Européenne, Paris, Descartes & Cie, 1997

LACROIX Guy, *Le mirage Internet, enjeux économiques et sociaux*; Paris, VIGOT, Collection Essentiel, 1997

LESSIG Lawrence, *Code And Other laws of cyberspace*, NY, Basic Books, 1999

162

Bibliography

LEVY Pierre, *Cyberculture, rapport au conseil de l'Europe dans le cadre du projet "Nouvelles technologies: coopération culturelle et communication"*, Paris, Editions Odile Jacob, Edition du Conseil de l'Europe, 1977

LEVY Pierre, *World Philosophie*, Paris, Odile JACOB, COLLECTION "CHAMPS MÉDIOLOGIQUE", 2000

MATTELART Armand, *La mondialisation de la communication*, Paris PUF, Que sais-je?, 1996

O'DONNELL James J., *Avatars Of The Word, From Papyrus To Cyberspace*, Cambridge, Mass., Harvard University Press, 1998

OECD, *France's Experience With The Minitel: Lessons For Electronic Commerce Over The Internet*, DSTI/ICCP/ie (97) 10/FINAL, http://www.ocde.org.

QUITTNER Joshua and SLATALLA Michelle, *Speeding the net*, London, Orion Business Books, 1998

RINCE Jean-Yves, *Le Minitel*, Paris, PUF, Que Sais-je?, n° 2539, 1990

STEFIK Mark, *The Internet Edge, Social, Legal and Technological Challenges for a Networked World*, MIT, 1999

WHINSTON Andrew B., STAHL Dale O., CHOI Soon-Yong, *The Economics of Electronic Commerce,* Indianapolis, Indiana, Macmillan Technical Publishing, 1997

WOLTON Dominique, *Internet et après? Une théorie critique des nouveaux médias*, Paris Flammarion, 1999

ON THE CONCEPT OF TERRITORY

ALLIÈS Paul, *L'invention du territoire,* Grenoble, 1980

ANDREFF Wladimir, "La déterritorialisation des multi-nationales: firmes globales et firmes réseaux", in *L'international sans territoire*, Paris, L'Harmattan, 1996, pp. 373-396.

ARDEN Harvey, *Noble Red Man, Mathew King, un sage Lakota*, translated by Karin BODSON, Paris, Editions du Rocher, 1994

163

BROMLEY Nicholas K., *Law, Space and the Geographies of Power*, New York, 1994.

FLORY Maurice, "Le couple Etat-territoire en droit international contemporain", in *L'international sans territoire,* Paris, L'Harmattan, 1996, pp. 251-265.

MAGNANT Jean-Pierre, *Terre et pouvoir dans les populations dites "Sara" du Sud du Tchad*, Paris I, thesis political sciences, 1983

MERLE Marcel, "Un système international sans territoire?", *L'international sans territoire*, L'Harmattan, 1996, pp. 289-309

MOLYNEAUX Brian Leigh, *The Sacred Earth*, London, Macmillan, 1995

OTIS Ghislain et MELKEVICK Bjarne, "L'universalisme moderne à l'heure des identités: le défi singulier des peuples autochtones", in *Les Droits Fondamentaux*, BRUXELLES, BRUYLANT 1997, ACTES des 1ères Journées scientifiques du Réseau Droits fondamentaux de l'AUPELF-UREF

PELT Jean-Marie, *La vie sociale des plantes*, Paris, Fayard, 2ème édition, 1984

VERHOEVEN Joe, "Souveraineté et mondialisation: libres propos", in La mondialisation du droit, under the direction of Eric LOQUIN et Catherine KESSEDJIAN, Travaux du Centre de Recherche sur le droit des marchés et des investissements internationaux, book 19, Paris LITEC, 2000, pp. 43-57

LAW AND THEORY OF LAW

ABERKANE Hassen, *Contribution à l'étude de la distinction des droits de créance et des droits réels*, Paris, LGDJ, 1957

BOITEUX, *Commentaire sur le Code Napoléon*, Paris, 6e édition, 1852

BOQUET Claude, *De l'opposabilité aux tiers comme caractéristique du droit réel: essai d'épistémologie juridique sur la base des droits allemand, français et suisse;* Genève, Avenir, 1978

CAPITANT Henri, *Introduction à l'étude du droit civil*, Paris, 1904

CATALA (P), "La transformation du patrimoine dans le droit civil moderne", Revue. trimestrielle. droit. civil, 1966

CLAVIER Jean-Pierre, *Les catégories de la propriété intellectuelle à l'épreuve des créations génétiques*, Paris et Montréal, L'Harmattan, 1998

Court TV: http://www.courttv.com/old/library/cyberlaw/ny_decency.

DABIN Jean, "Les droits intellectuels comme catégorie juridique" Paris, Revue critique de législation et de jurisprudence, 1939

DABIN Jean, "Les droits intellectuels comme catégorie juridique", Revue critique de législation et de jurisprudence, 1939

DELVINCOURT, *Cours de droit civil*, Paris, 1825

DEMOGUE René, *Les notions fondamentales du droit privé, Essai critique pour servir d'introduction à l'étude des obligations*, Paris, Rousseau, 1911

DEMOLOMBE, *Cours de Code Napoléon*, Paris, 1854

DERUPPÉ Jean, *La nature juridique du droit du preneur à bail et la distinction des droits réels et des droits de créance*, Paris, Dalloz, 1952

DURANTON Alexandre, *Cours de droit français*, 2e édition, Paris, 8e édition, 1828

EBKE Werner F., FINKIN Matthew W., *Introduction to German law*, The Hague, London, Boston, Kluwer Law International, 1996

GINOSSAR Samuel, *Droit réel, propriété et créance - élaboration d'un système rationnel des droits patrimoniaux*, Paris, LGDJ, 1960

GUILLIEN Raymond et VINCENT Jean, *Lexique des termes juridiques*, Paris, Dalloz, 1988

JOSSERAND Louis, "Configuration du droit de propriété dans l'ordre juridique nouveau", *Mélanges juridiques, dédiés à Monsieur le Professeur SUGIYAMA*, TOKIO 1940

KRUSE Frederik Vinding, *The Right of Property*, London, New

Bibliography

York, Toronto, Oxford University Press, 1939

LESENNE, *De la propriété avec ses démembrements*, Paris, 1858

LEVIS Marc, *l'Opposabilité du droit réel*, Paris II, thesis, 1985

Lois et Actes du Gouvernement, book 1, Paris, Imprimerie Royale, 1834

MARCADé, *Explication du code civil*, Paris, 1886

MARTY (G) et RAYNAUD (P), *Droit civil, Introduction générale à l'étude du droit*, Paris, SIREY, 1972

MICHAS H., *Le droit réel considéré comme une obligation passivement universelle*, Paris, thesis.1900

MOURLON ET DEMANGEAT, *Répétitions écrites sur le code civil*, Paris, 1896

PICARD Edmond, *Le droit pur - Cours d'Encyclopédie du droit- les permanences juridiques abstraites*, Paris, Edition Félix Alcan, 1899

PLANIOL Marcel, *Traité élémentaire de droit civil*, Paris, Pichon, 1908

POUILLET Eugène, *Traité théorique et pratique de la propriété littéraire et artistique et du droit de représentation*, Paris, Marchal et Billard, 1908

POTHIER, *OEUVRES*, Paris, 1847, book IX, "Traité du droit de domaine de propriété"

PRODAN C., *Essai d'une théorie générale des droits réels*, Paris, Thesis, 1909

QUERU R., *Synthèse du droit réel et du droit personnel - Essai d'une critique historique et théorique du réalisme juridique*, Caen, Thesis, 1905

RENO v. ACLU, 26 juin 1997, n° 96-511, *cf.*
http://www.aclu.org/issues/cyber/trial/sctran.html
Text of the *Communications Decency act*:http://www.epic.org/cda/cda
Other documents: http://www.epic.org/cda
RIGAUD Louis, *Le droit réel, histoire et théories, son origine*

institutionnelle, Toulouse, thesis, 1912

RIPERT Georges, *De l'exercice du droit de propriété dans ses rapports avec les propriétés voisines*, Aix, thesis, 1902

ROLAND Henri, BOYER Laurent, *Adages du droit français*, Paris, Litec, 1999

ROUBIER Paul, *Droits subjectifs et situations juridiques*, Paris, Dalloz, 1963

TERRÉ François, *Introduction Générale au Droit*, Paris, Dalloz, 4ème édition, 1998

TERRÉ François, *Introduction Générale au Droit*, Paris, Dalloz, 4ème édition, 1998

TERRÉ François, SIMLER Philippe, LEQUETTE Yves, *Droit civil, les obligations*, Paris, Dalloz, 1999

TOULLIER Charles, *Le droit civil français*, Paris, 1830

VAN BEMMELEN, *les notions fondamentales du droit civil*, Amsterdam, 1892

VERHOEVEN Joe, "Souveraineté et mondialisation: libres propos", in La mondialisation du droit, under the direction of Eric LOQUIN et Catherine KESSEDJIAN, Travaux du Centre de Recherche sur le droit des marchés et des investissements internationaux, book 19, Paris, LITEC, 2000, pp. 43-57

VILLEY Michel, "La notion romaine classique de *Jus* et le *Dikaion* d'Aristote", La filosofia greca e il diritto romano, Roma, Accademia Nazionale dei Lincei, 1976, pp. 71-79

VILLEY Michel, "Les origines de la notion de droit subjectif", *Archives de Philosophie du Droit*, Paris, Recueil SIREY, 1953-54, pp. 163-187.

VOIRIN Pierre, *Droit civil*, book 1, Paris, L.G.D.J., 1999

WIPO, Copyright Treaty, Geneva, December 1996, article 6. Http://www.wipo.org

Bibliography

PHILOSOPHY AND PHILOSOPHY OF LAW

ARISTOTLE, *The Nicomachean ethics*; with an English translation by H. Rackman, Cambridge, Mass.: Harvard University Press; London: W. Heinemann, 1947

BOISTEL, *Cours de philosophie du droit*, Paris, 2 books, 1899

HERVADA Javier, *Introduction critique au droit naturel*, Bordeaux, EDITIONS BIERE, 1991

JASPERS Karl, *Origine et sens de l'histoire*, traduit de l'Allemand par Hélène NAEF, avec la collaboration de Wolfgang ACHTERBERG, Paris, Plon, 1954 German original title: Von Urprung un Ziel der Geschitchte

KANT Emmanuel, *Métaphysique des moeurs, Première partie, Doctrine du Droit*, Paris, Vrin, 1993; KANT Immanual, The science of right, translated by W. HASTIE, http://www.eserver.org

KELSEN Hans, *Théorie Pure du Droit, Introduction à la Science du Droit*, Neuchatel, Editions de la Baconnière, Juin 1953 traduit de l'allemand par Henri Thévenaz, titre allemand *Reine Rechtslehre*

KIERKEGAARD Sören, *Traité du désespoir*, Traduit du danois par Knud FERLOV et Jean-Jacques GATEAU, Paris, Gallimard, Folio Essais, 1949; KIERKEGAARD Sören, *The concept of Dread*, translated by Walter LOWRIE, Princeton, Princeton university Press, 1967

MELKEVIK Bjarne, *Horizons de la philosophie du droit*, L'Harmattan, Paris, Montréal, PUL, 1998

RAWLS John, *A theory Of Justice*, Cambridge, Mass., Belknap Press of Harvard University Press, 1971

ROUSSEAU Jean-Jacques, *Discours sur les Sciences et les Arts, Discours sur l'Origine de l'Inégalité*, Paris, GARNIER-PLAMMARION, 1971; ROUSSEAU Jean-Jacques, *Discourse on the origin of inequality,* translated by Franklin PHILIP, Oxford, NY, Oxford University Press, 1994

TRIGEAUD Jean-Marc, *Persona ou la justice au double visage*, Genova, Studio Editoriale di Cultura, 1997

TZITZIS Stamatios, *Esthétique de la Violence*, Paris, PUF, 1997

TZITZIS Stamatios, *Qu'est-ce que la personne?* Paris, Armand Colin, 1999

ANCIENT ROMAN LAW

BREAL Michel and BAILLY Anatole, *Dictionnaire étymologique latin*, Paris, Hachette, 1898

CATALANO Pierangelo, *Diritto e Personne, Studi su origine e attualità del sistema romano*, Torino, G. GIAPAICHELLI EDITORE, 1990

GAUDEMET Jean, *Droit privé romain*, Paris, Montchrestien, 2000

GRIMAL Pierre, *La civilisation romaine*, Paris, Champs, Flammarion, 1997

GUARINO Antonio, *Storia del diritto romano*, Napoli, Jovene, 1998

HUVELIN Paul, *Les tablettes magiques et le droit romain*, Macon, Protat Frères, 1901

JHERING von R., *L'esprit du droit romain dans les diverses phases de son développement*, translation by O. de MEULENAERE, Paris, Librairie A. Marescq, MDCCCLXXXVI

LEVY-BRUHL Henri, *Droit romain*, Paris, Cours de droit, 1955/56.

LEVY-BRUHL Henri, *Le très ancien procès romain*, Rome, 1952

.

LEVY-BRUHL Henri, *Nouvelles Etudes sur le Très Ancien Droit romain*, Paris, Recueil SIREY, 1947

LEVY-BRUHL Henri, *Recherches sur les actions de la loi*, Paris, Recueil Sirey, 1960

PARICIO Javier, FERNANDEZ BARREIRO A., *Historia del derecho romano y su reception europea*, Madrid, Editorial centro de estudios Ramon Areces, 1995.

POTTER T. W., *Roman Britain*, London, Bristish Museum Press, 1997

169

Bibliography

REVILLOUT Eugène, *Les origines égyptiennes du droit civil romain*, Paris, Librairie Paul Geuthner, 1912

VILLEY Michel: "Le jus in re du droit romain classique au droit moderne", in Publications de l'Institut de droit romain de l'Université de Paris, 1947, p. 193

VILLEY Michel, "Historique de la nature des choses", Paris, Archives de Philosophie du droit, book X, 1965, pp. 267-283.

VILLEY Michel, "Métamorphoses de l'obligation", *Archives de Philosophie du droit*, Communication au congrès de l'Institut International de Philosophie politique sur "l'obligation politique", 4 July 1969

VILLEY Michel, *Le Droit Romain*, PUF, Que sais-je?, 7e édition, 1979

VILLEY Michel, *Suum jus cuique tribuens*, Milano, Giuffré, 1954

EGYPTOLOGY AND HISTORY OF RELIGIONS

AMÉLINEAU Emile, *La morale égyptienne quinze siècles avant notre ère, Etude sur le papyrus de Boulaq n° 4*, Paris, Editions Ernest Leroux, 1892

ASSMANN Jan, *Maât, l'Egypte pharaonique et l'idée de justice sociale*, Conférences essais et leçons du Collège de France, Paris, Julliard, 1989

BICKEL S., *La cosmogonie égyptienne avant le Nouvel Empire*, Fribourg, 1999

BLEEKER Claas Jouco, *De Beteekenis van de Egyptische Godin Ma-a-t*, Leiden, 1929

BLEEKER Claas Jouco, *Egyptians Festivals, Enactments Of Religious Renewal*, Leiden, Netherlands, E.J. Brill, 1967

BLEIBERG Edward, *The official Gift In Ancient Egypt*, Oklahoma, University of Oklahoma Press, 1996

CHAMPOLLION, *L'Egypte de Jean-François CHAMPOLLION*,

170

ouvrage collectif, Paris, Mengès, 1998

DERCHAIN Philippe, *Le papyrus Salt 825 (BM 10051) rituel pour la conservation de la vie en Egypte*, Bruxelles, Académie royale de Belgique, Mémoire n° 1784, Classe des lettres, book LVIII, fasc. I a, 1965

DRIOTON Etienne, "Le jugement des âmes dans l'Egypte ancienne", Revue du Caire, 1949, pp. 1-20

FAULKNER R.O., *The Ancient Egyptian Book Of The Dead*, London, British Museum, 1996

FRANKFORT H, FRANKFORT A, WILSON, JACOBSON AND IRWIN, *The Intellectual Adventure Of Ancient Man*, Chicago, University of Chicago Press, 1946

FRANKFORT Henri, *Ancient Egyptian Religion, An Interpretation*, New York, Columbia University Press, 1948

FRANKFORT Henri, *Kingship And The Gods*, Chicago, 1948

GOFF Beatrice L., *Symbols Of Ancient Egypt In The Late Period, The Twenty-first Dynasty*, Yale University, Mouton publishers, 1979

GOYON Jean-Claude, *Maât et Pharaon ou le destin de l'Egypte antique*, Lyon, Editions ACV, 1998

GRIMAL Pierre, in Claire LALOUETTE, *Textes sacrés et Textes profanes de l'Ancienne Egypte*, book I, *Des Pharaons et des Hommes*, 1984, Gallimard/Unesco, p. 8 and p. 16

HERODOTE, *L'Enquête*, Book I to IV, édition d'Andrée BARQUET, Paris, Gallimard, Folio classique, 1964

HORNUNG Erik, *L'esprit du temps des pharaons*, Paris, Hachette, collection Pluriel, 1996

IVERSEN Erik, *The Myth Of Egypt And Its Hieroglyphs in European Tradition*, Copenhagen, GEC Gad, 1961

LALOUETTE Claire, *Textes sacrés et Textes profanes de l'Ancienne Egypte*, book I: *Des Pharaons et des Hommes*, Paris, Gallimard/Unesco, 1984

Bibliography

LALOUETTE Claire, *Textes sacrés et Textes profanes de l'Ancienne Egypte, book II: Mythes, contes et poésies*, Paris, Gallimard/Unesco, 1987

LICHTHEIM Myriam, *Maat In Egyptian Autobiographies And Related Studies*, Fribourg, Universitätsverlag Freiburg Schweiz, Vandenthoeck and Ruprecht Göttingen, 1992

MENU Bernadette, "Le tombeau de Pétosiris (2) Maât, Thot et le droit", Paris, BIFAO (Bulletin de l'Institut Français d'Archéologie Orientale), book 95 (1995), pp. 281-295

MORENZ Siegfried, *Egyptian Religion*, London, Methuen and Co litd, 1976

MORET Alexandre, "La doctrine de Maât", Revue d'Egyptologie, book 4, Imprimerie de l'Institut français d'Archéologie Orientale, Le Caire, 1940, pp. 1-14

MORET Alexandre, "Le jugement des morts, en Egypte et hors d'Egypte", Paris, Annales du Musée GUIMET, book XXXII, pp. 255-287

MORET Alexandre, *Le Nil et la civilisation égyptienne*, Paris, La Renaissance du livre, 1926

MORET Alexandre, *Rituel du culte divin journalier en Egypte*, Paris, Ernest Leroux, 1902

PIANKOFF Alexandre, *Le "coeur" dans les textes égyptiens*, Paris, Librairie Paul Geuthner, 1930

RACHET Guy, *Le livre des morts des anciens Égyptiens*, Paris, Editions du Rocher, 1996

REVILLOUT Eugène, *Les origines égyptiennes du droit civil romain*, Paris, Librairie Paul Geuthner, 1912

SARRAF Joseph, *La notion du droit d'après les Anciens Egyptiens*, Rome, Città del Vaticano, Libreria editrice vaticana, 1984, Collana storia e attualità, No 10

 [end]

SHAW Ian and NICHOLSON Paul, *Dictionary Of Ancient Egypt*, London, British Museum Press, 1995

SHIRUN-GRUMACH Irene, "Remarks on the Goddess MAAT", *Pharaonic Egypt, The Bible And Christianity*, Jerusalem, ed. S. Israelit-Groll, the Magnes Press, The Hebrew University, 1985, 173-201

SHUPAK Nili, "Some idioms connected with the concept of 'heart' in Egypt and the Bible", *Pharaonic Egypt, The Bible And Christianity*, Jerusalem, éd. S. Israelit-Groll, the Magnes Press, The Hebrew University, 1985, 202-212

TEETER Emily, *The Presentation Of Maat, Ritual and Legitimacy in Ancient Egypt*, Chicago, The University of Chicago, 1997

WILSON Hilary, *Understanding Hieroglyphs*, London, Brockhampton Press, 1999

YOYOTTE Jean, Entretien avec, "L'échange est au coeur de la civilisation égyptienne", *Eurêka*, Paris, BAYARD PRESSE, Septembre 1998, n° 35

YOYOTTE Jean, "La pensée préphilosophique en Egypte", extr. Encyclopédie de la Pléiade, histoire de la philosophie, I, Paris 19.., pp.1-23

YOYOTTE Jean, "Le jugement des morts selon l'Egypte ancienne", Paris, Sources Orientales, IV, 1961, pp. 17-71

Bibliography

Also by Anna MANCINI:

ANCIENT ROMAN SOLUTIONS TO MODERN LEGAL ISSUES
THE EXAMPLE OF PATENT LAW

Our Law and its philosophy have been conceived for an economic world where the main source of wealth was material. Although this world no longer exists, its laws are still alive and slow down the development of modern economies. Patent law strikingly shows this fact. Invented mainly during the industrial revolution in order to protect tangible inventions, it could not be applied to the new intangible inventions of the 20th century. Software, for example, has been denied protection under patent law, due to its lack of materiality. Since such a cause of denial is economically absurd, we should adapt patent law to the virtual world. This was not done and so no new intangible invention can benefit from this protection through a lack of tangibility. Long before us, the ancient Romans had understood that the intangible world and the material world do not function the same way. Since they were very practical people, they took this reality into account to build their legal system. Their legal experience has become valuable for a modern world that is rediscovering the value of ideas and people's wealth, too long eclipsed by materialism.

Anna MANCINI, Ph. D.

Categories: Law, Patent Law, Philosophy of Law, Roman Law

ISBN: 1-932848-04-5 (paperback)
ISBN: 1-932848-05-3 (E-book)

Also by Anna MANCINI

Maat Revealed, Philosophy of Justice

in Ancient Egypt

Unlike ancient Rome, Egypt did not transmit any legal system to us, but rather an idea of justice our modern minds can hardly understand. In the ancient Egyptian world, almost all the texts and inscriptions speak of justice. All the texts of wisdom teach that one has to conform to Maat, an obscure and omnipresent concept that Egyptologists have translated into the expression "Goddess of Truth and Justice".

Egyptian justice is so different from ours that Egyptologists and historians of religions believe they have not yet fully understood its meaning. They regret this fact because understanding Maat would be a gateway to a deeper understanding of the ancient Egyptian world. As for lawyers, they have limited themselves to the Greco-Roman sources on the philosophy of Justice and the discoveries of Egyptologists in this philosophical field remain thoroughly ignored. Thanks to her experience in ancient history of law and her ability to understand ancient symbols, the author provides Egyptology with the missing pieces that were needed to form a coherent image of Maat. Once revealed, Maat sheds a new and unexpected light on the whole of Egyptian civilization. As a bridge between traditionally separate fields of academic research, this book is a useful and groundbreaking contribution to Egyptology, the history of religions and the modern philosophy of law.

Categories: Egyptology, philosophy of law, history of religions

Price : 25 USD

Buenos Books America
WWW. BUENOSBOOKSAMERICA.COM

1-932848-10-X Paperback Maat Reveale, 132 pages
1-932848-11-8 E-Book MAAT REVEALED

www.ingramcontent.com/pod-product-compliance
Lightning Source LLC
Chambersburg PA
CBHW051237050326
40689CB00007B/965